THE CHURCH OF OUR FATHERS

BY
ROLAND H. BAINTON

NEW YORK
CHARLES SCRIBNERS SONS
1944

THIS BOOK IS DEDICATED TO OLIVE HERBERT JOYCE CEDRIC AND RUTH

CONTENTS

vi CONTENTS

THE CHURCH OF OUR FATHERS

THE BEGINNINGS OF THE CHURCH

HE Church is our spiritual home. In every village and town the skyline is marked by the slender spire or the square tower of the church. In Europe and America the Church has been the greatest force in shaping the world in which we live. Universities, schools and colleges, hospitals and asylums, better prisons, kinder laws, the ending of slavery and duelling and the attempt to end war and bring in the brotherhood of man, all these have been in large measure the work of the Church.

The Church is something like a tree whose limbs branch off some small, some large; some straight, some twisted; and whose leaves in the fall may be still mostly green with patches here and there of gold and flame. Even so the Church has many branches and leaves differing as to the form of the building, the dress of the clergy, the services and beliefs. Some spires are tipped with crosses and some with weather vanes. Some churches give the altar a central position in front, and some the pulpit. In some the minister wears robes of many colors, in others only a plain suit. The Quakers have no altars and no pulpit and no minister. Yet all have one God, one Master, and one Spirit.

This book will try to tell briefly the story of the Christian Church, how it came to be in the days of Jesus, and how in many forms it has continued until now. The story will be told in part by the use of pictures drawn close to the time of the events which they describe. In some cases, of course, no drawing was made at the time. We have no trustworthy likenesses of Jesus or Peter or Paul. The earliest pictures we have of them were drawn more than a hundred years after they were dead. Sometimes pictures of Bible scenes have been used to show how the people looked who drew the pictures, for the artists dressed the Bible characters the way they dressed themselves.

On the page opposite are six pictures of David and Goliath, each drawn a hundred years or more after the other. The first shows a stone carving of Goliath as a Roman soldier. An arm has been broken off. Next he appears as a soldier of Charlemagne, then as a Saxon, and then as a Crusader in a coat of mail. Close to the time of the discovery of America he is shown in plate armor. The last picture was made after the invention of gunpowder, which made armor of little use. The stomach of this Goliath is quite unprotected. Such pictures help us to understand the people who drew them.

Our story starts in the time of Jesus. He was born in Palestine two thousand years ago, and was brought up in the Jewish religion, described in our Old Testament. His father was a carpenter, and Jesus, as a boy, helped in the shop. When he was thirty, a religious teacher like one of the old Jewish prophets appeared in the desert, telling men to be sorry for their sins because God was about to bring in a new age. This was John the

Baptist. He was called the Baptist because he baptized. Jesus was baptized by him and then became a teacher in Galilee, the northern part of Palestine.

The common people heard him gladly because he lightened the burden of their religion by giving up the petty rules of the Pharisees, the students of the Jewish law, who would not allow the hungry when passing through a field of corn to do even the work of rubbing off the husks in their hands if the day were the Sabbath. Jesus said, "The Sabbath was made for man and not man for the Sabbath." He made religion more simple and sensible, but not easier, for he taught men to forgive injuries and love even enemies. He cured people of diseases. Great crowds followed him and listened with gladness to his words. Some even wished to make him a king.

Jesus gathered about him a little band of followers and called them to be "fishers of men." They were the beginning of the Christian Church. The Greek word for church, *ecclesia*, means "those who are called." From this comes the Italian, *chiesa*, and French, *église*. The English word *church*, like the Scotch *kirk* and the German *Kirche*, comes from another Greek word, *kuriake*, meaning "the Lord's" (house).

One might have supposed that a person so good and kind and great as Jesus would have had everybody on his side, but such was not the case. The Pharisees disliked him from the start because he broke their rules. The common people turned away because he would not use his power to drive out the Roman conquerors who held Judæa in rough bondage. The Jews believed that God would send a Messiah, which means an anointed one, to deliver them. Might not Jesus be that Messiah? Could he not gather the people and drive out the Romans? Jesus was indeed a Messiah sent by God, but not to take the sword against the enemy. He was to set up his kingdom in the hearts of men. When the common people found that he would not lead them in a war of rebellion they turned against him.

The rich came to fear him for a different reason. They did not mind if he changed the rules for the Sabbath. Nor did they wish a war against the Romans under whose rule they were doing well. But Jesus angered them by attacking a practice which had grown up in the temple at Jerusalem. Here stood a great altar, that is a stone on which animals are killed as an offering to God. The Jews who came up to the temple from all parts of the world could not bring with them the oxen, lambs and doves to sacrifice and had to buy them on the spot. The money which they brought with them was not of the right kind and had to be changed into the coinage of the temple. The sellers of the animals and the changers of the money made a big profit which went into the purses of the rich. This business was going on in the very temple itself. Jesus drove out the men and animals and overturned the tables of money.

Three groups hated him then: the strict keepers of the law, those of the common people wishing to rebel, and the rich. All watched for a chance to take him. Jesus, knowing that he could not long be hidden, had a Last Supper with his disciples, and pointed to the bread and wine upon the table as signs of his body and blood which would be broken on the morrow. All would desert him, he foretold, but Peter roundly stated that no matter what others might do, he would not fail. "Before the cock crows," said Jesus, "you will say three times that you do not know me."

After supper they went to the Garden of Gethsemane, where Jesus was taken by the Roman soldiers. The disciples fled. Peter followed at a distance. A servant girl pointed him out as a follower

of Jesus. He swore that he did not know him. Three times he swore. The cock crew. Peter went out and wept.

Jesus was brought before the Roman governor, Pilate, and was accused of starting a revolt against Rome. That was exactly what he would not do, but the Romans were afraid of any disturbance and did not look too closely at what it was all about. Jesus was condemned and put to death upon a cross. In his pain, he prayed for his tormentors, "Father, forgive them, for they know not what they do."

Jesus was laid in a tomb. The disciples had fled.

To Peter first came the assurance that Jesus was not dead. He still lived. Some had seen him. Others had not, but they, too, were sure, because of what they saw happening. Those who before had lived for themselves, who had fought their enemies and quarrelled with their friends, who had left their wives and cast off their children, now were changed men. A strange new power was at work among them—the Spirit of Jesus in their midst.

The earliest pictures by the Christians show their beliefs. Many of these pictures are found in the catacombs, underground passages only three feet wide, winding in a maze beneath the surface of the outskirts of Rome. The catacombs were the cemeteries of the Christians. The word catacomb means a place of sleeping underground and the word cemetery also means a sleeping place because the Christians believed that death is only a sleep. Along the walls of the catacombs were ledges for the remains of the dead, and on the bare spaces were carved names and words and pictures. Other pictures are on vases, lamps, and rings.

Jonah was the sign of the risen Jesus. Our Lord himself was not portrayed rising from the grave, but Jonah appeared instead. This was because the Gospel of Matthew said that as Jonah was three days and three nights inside the whale, so should Jesus be that long buried in the earth until he should rise from the dead. Jesus himself was shown as the Good Shepherd caring for the lamb. The face of the shepherd is not the one with the beard that came to be used for Jesus. We do not know what he looked like. Signs which stand for him are the first two letters of his name in Greek. Our CH was one letter in Greek and was shaped like our X; and the Greek R had the shape of our P. These two letters were combined in a monogram. Also the first and last letters of the Greek alphabet, called alpha and omega, stand for Jesus, because he is the first and the last. The dove stands for the spirit of God, and also for peace. The fish was a common sign of Christianity because Jesus had fed the multitude with loaves and fishes, because he told the disciples to be fishers of men, and because the letters of the word for fish in Greek contained the first letters of the Greek words meaning, "Jesus Son of God Savior."

Peter, sure that Christ was alive, gathered the disciples and began preaching to the people that Jesus, who was crucified, still lived. Let them be sorry for their wrongdoing and turn and follow him. The Jewish leaders told Peter to stop. He answered, "Decide for yourselves whether it is right for me to obey you or God." A leader of the Jews, very hot against the Christians, was called Saul. He gained an order from the priests at Jerusalem to go to Damascus and hunt out the Christians. On the way, he was struck as by a light from heaven and became a Christian himself. Then he took the name of Paul. Here is an early picture of him. In later times he was commonly pictured with a sword and a book.

Paul had been angry with the Christians because they would not keep the Jewish law. When he became a Christian, he decided that the Jewish law was not necessary at all and should be given up entirely. The other disciples agreed that the law was not absolutely necessary, yet they continued to keep most of it. If Paul were right, non-Jews, who were called Gentiles, could join the Christian Church without having to keep the law of the Jews. There were debates over this question in the early Church. Paul won, and went out to be a great preacher to the Gentiles.

In the Greek cities and in Rome, Paul preached Christ crucified and risen from the dead. The Jews, of course, opposed him, because this was not their belief. The Gentiles also opposed him because they worshipped idols, or images of their gods, which Paul said were no gods and should be broken. The men who made their livings by carving the idols naturally did not like such teachings. At Ephesus they staged a riot.

The Roman governors could not overlook disturbances of this sort. They did not care what caused them. The Roman was not interested in disputes about the Jewish law and not especially in the idols of the Greeks, but riots must be stopped. As Paul seemed to be the cause of the riots he was frequently imprisoned and beaten. After a long imprisonment at Rome he was put to death.

The Romans at first did not understand that Christianity was a different religion from that of the Jews. Jesus had been a Jew. Paul was a Jew. Their religion, then, must be a form of Judaism. But as time went on the Romans were to find that Christianity was a new religion, a religion which grew stronger every day, a religion which would overturn many beliefs and practices of the Roman Empire, a religion which could not be overlooked.

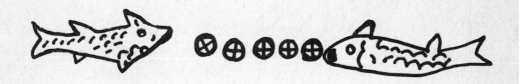

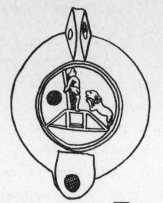

CHAPTER TWO

TRIAL BY FIRE

ERRIBLE testing was now ahead for the Christians. The Roman Empire was large and powerful and at that time included a great part of the known world. The Empire was governed by an Emperor, regarded by the Romans as a god. In this picture the Emperor, Marcus Aurelius, and his wife, Faustina, are being borne to heaven by eagles and also by a winged figure like an angel. In the right-hand corner of the picture is the goddess of Rome. On her shield are the twins, Romulus and Remus, founders of Rome, with the wolf by whom they were brought up.

The Romans were willing to worship their Emperor and to burn incense on his altar. The Christians refused. The Romans served as soldiers and defended their Empire against barbarian

10

tribes. The Christians had been taught by Christ to love their enemies and for that reason were unwilling to serve in the army. Many other things, too, common in Roman society they would not do. The Romans thus discovered that Christianity was a new religion and from their point of view a very dangerous one. The rulers began to punish the Christians.

Something about how and why, we learn from a letter of one of the governors in the provinces to the Emperor Trajan. The letter was written about a hundred years after Christ. The governor said, "I do not know just what to do with the Christians for I have never been present at one of their trials. Shall I punish boys and girls as severely as grown ups? Is just being a Christian enough to punish or must something bad actually have been done? If the accused says he is not a Christian, shall I let him go? What I have done, in the case of those who admitted they were Christians, was to order them sent to Rome, if citizens; if not to have them killed. I was sure they deserved to be punished because they were so stubborn. I gave them three chances to save themselves by putting incense on your altar and cursing Christ. I have heard a real Christian will not do that. The Christians claim that they do nothing worse than to meet before dawn on a certain day and sing hymns to Christ. They promise not to steal or lie. They also meet for a common meal (the Lord's Supper), though they have given this up since my order against secret meetings. I had some women slaves called deaconesses tortured, but could not find out anything worse than some crazy ideas. Many people had been touched by this foolishness and the temples were nearly empty, but now the people are coming back."

Such treatment seems to us very cruel. But we must be fair and try to imagine how the Christians appeared to the Romans. So many things which other people did Christians would not do. Such things often were not wrong in themselves, but became wrong for the Christians because of a connection with heathen religion.

One would have supposed that the Christian could see no harm in going to a hospital. Nor would he, except that the pagan hospitals were under the protection of the heathen god, Æsculapius, and while the sick man lay in his bed, the priest went down the aisle chanting to the god. One would have assumed that the Christian would have had no difficulty in going to school. Nor would he, except that the school books told stories about the pagan gods, not just as stories, but as true.

Even a Christian sculptor found himself in difficulties, for he would almost surely be called on to make idols for the pagans. Here is a picture of a funeral stone set up by a Christian sculptor in honor of his father, who is shown with his hands in the position then in common use for prayer. The Greek words mean, "Blessed Eutropius, a worshipper of God. May you rest in peace. Made by his son. Buried ten days before the first of September." The sculptor is shown making lions' heads. On another stone he has carved whales. A Christian could do this, but lions and whales by themselves were not easy to sell. The pagans wanted, in addition, carvings of their gods. But when these were ordered, the Christian sculptor had to say no.

Some things the Christians would not do because these things seemed wrong in themselves. They would not go to the gladiatorial combats in which the Romans, just for the amusement of the crowd, forced prisoners of war and slaves to fight with each other to the death. The Christians would not go to the theatre because the plays were cruel and coarse. The Christians would not go to the law court since the Apostle Paul had said that when Christians quarrelled they should settle things among themselves. The practice grew up of letting the bishop decide disputes. He sat in a chair called a *cathedra*. Later when the chair was placed in a church that church was called a cathedral. In the picture you may see a *cathedra* with a dove perched upon it. The dove stands for the Spirit of God teaching the bishop to decide what is right.

Then the Christians for a long time would not go to war. They kept slaves but treated them kindly and permitted them to have the same rights within the church as any one else. A former slave became the bishop of Rome. Christians, unlike the pagans, would not take weak or unwanted children out in the woods and leave them to die or be picked up by robbers. If a Christian woman was married to a pagan and a girl baby was born, the father might say, "Throw her out," but the mother would refuse. If the Christian wife died she would be buried by the Christians in their catacombs, away from the burial place of her husband.

One can see why the pagans thought of the Christians as stubborn and queer, even as "enemies of mankind." Soon many untrue stories were told about the Christians which made the hatred of the pagans all the greater. The Emperor Nero charged the Christians with setting fire to Rome. He really did it himself, but shifted the blame to the Christians and had them nailed to crosses and covered with pitch and burned in his gardens as torches by night.

The crowds began to pass around the silly story that the Christians worshipped a donkey's head. Some pagan scratched this drawing on a wall in Rome. The words mean, "Alexamenos worships his god." The language is Greek, for the Greeks had moved to Rome in great numbers.

Worse charges, too, were brought against the Christians. They were said to be cannibals and to eat babies. This story started because the Lord's Supper was practised in secret. The heathen did not know what happened at these secret meetings but they heard that somebody was being eaten. Jesus had said at the Last Supper, "This bread is my body. This wine is my blood." Very well then, said the pagans, the Christians must be eating and drinking human flesh and blood.

The mobs thought that people who did such terrible things, if allowed to live, would bring all manner of trouble on the land. Such wickedness would stir up the gods, who would punish, not only the Christians, but those who had allowed them to exist. When the cattle died or the river Tiber overflowed its banks, the pagans said, "See! Let's throw the Christians to the lions."

We have a case of this sort at Smyrna in what is now Turkey. The time was about a hundred and fifty years after Christ. The mob began crying, "Away with the atheists!" (those who do not believe in the gods). "Get Polycarp." Polycarp, who was the aged bishop of Smyrna, wanted to give himself up, but friends persuaded him to go out to a little farm in the country. There he was caught and brought back to Smyrna. The High Sheriff, whose own sister happened to be a Christian, talked to Polycarp as they rode into the city together. "What is the harm," he asked, "in saying, 'Cæsar is Lord' and putting the incense on his altar and saving yourself?"

Polycarp refused and was brought to the arena to be thrown to the lions. The officer gave him three chances to save his life. First he was ordered to say, "Away with the atheists!" Polycarp pointed to the heathen in the galleries and said, "Away with the atheists!" The governor gave him another chance, "Curse Christ." Polycarp answered, "Eighty and six years have I served him and he has done me no wrong, and can I revile my King that saved me?"

A third time the governor said, "Swear by Cæsar." Polycarp answered. "I am a Christian. If you want to know what that is, set a day and listen."

"Persuade the people," answered the governor. Polycarp said, "I would explain to you, but not to them."

"Then I'll throw you to the beasts." (The next picture shows a fragment of a Roman vase on which two men appear bound to stakes to be torn by beasts. The victims may not be Christians, but this is the way in which Christians were treated. A similar picture on a lamp appears at the head of this chapter.)

"Bring on your beasts," said Polycarp.

"If you scorn the beasts I'll have you burned."

"You try to frighten me with the fire that burns for an hour and you forget the fire of hell that never goes out."

The governor called to the people, "Polycarp says he is a Christian." Then the mob let loose, "This is the teacher of Asia," they shouted, "the father of the Christians, the destroyer of our gods."

Polycarp was burned at the stake. His dying prayer was, "Lord God, Almighty, Father of Jesus Christ, I bless Thee that Thou didst deem me worthy of this hour that I shall take a part among the martyrs in the cup of Christ to rise again with the Holy Spirit. May I be an acceptable sacrifice. I praise Thee, I bless Thee, I glorify Thee through Jesus Christ."

Thus far we have been considering mainly the struggle of Christianity with the government and with the mobs. Now we shall look at the other religions with which Christianity was in conflict. The gods of Greece and Rome best known to us are those who sat upon the sunny mountain top of Olympus. Some of these were Jupiter and Juno, Mercury, Venus, Mars, Saturn and Minerva. Five of these gave their names to the planets and one to a day of the week. Saturday is "Saturn's day."

Other gods also were popular in the Roman Empire, gods of the earth and the underworld such as Attis, Dionysus, Isis and

Osiris. The stories of these gods were myths explaining the dying and the rising of vegetation, the course of summer and winter. One of these myths is well known today, the story of Persephone or Proserpine. She was stolen from the earth by Pluto, the god of the underworld. Her mother Demeter or Ceres (from her name comes our word *cereal*) was the goddess of grain. While her daughter was away she would not let the grain grow. She tried to get Persephone back, but Pluto would consent only if she had eaten nothing while in the underworld. As it happened she had eaten the seeds of a pomegranate. Pluto went half way and let her return for six months of the year. This is the period of summer. When she is with him it is winter.

This story was something more than an explanation of the seasons. It was also a religion, because it promised that men might share not only in the dying but in the rising of the goddess. They tried by secret rites at her shrine to enter into her death and return to life. In the moonlight they wailed for the stolen goddess. At midnight they entered a cave and saw a play enacting her story. By this sight the people themselves were enabled like the goddess to overcome death.

Another of these religions was that of Mithras, the god of light. According to the legend Mithras killed a bull by stabbing

him in the flank. From the wound came grains of wheat. Here was a different explanation of the growth of vegetation, which was able to live because of the light and warmth from Mithras, the god of the sun. His birthday was on December 25th when the sun begins its upward course. And, as the sun comes back to life, so should those who believed in Mithras. His followers were men and often soldiers.

These religions had elements of good. They saw the hand of God in growing things. Christianity goes deeper because it sees the best working of God not in the dying and rising of the year, which is not really death but only seems to be, and cannot help itself, but rather in the dying of Jesus who went to a terrible death which he could have escaped and whose living spirit has ever since been seen at work in the changed lives of his followers.

Another type of religion in the Roman Empire was quite different and refused to see any signs of God in the world of nature. The world, said this religion, is bad. In it are flies and fleas and fevers. No good God would have made it. Our bodies are bad and the thing for us to do is to make them as miserable as we can until we can get rid of them. When people with these views became Christian they carried over some of their old ideas and said that, since the body is bad, and Jesus was good, he cannot have had a body, not a real one. Jesus, they said, was not really born, did not really suffer and die and rise. These people were called *Docetics* from a Greek word meaning to seem, because they said Jesus just seemed to have a body. They were also called *Gnostics* from the Greek word meaning "to know," because they said that the way to rise above the body is to know more. They were proud of all they knew and delighted in philosophies, astrology and magic.

The Church grew stronger and won out over the other religions partly because of the courageous way in which the Christians died, partly because of what they believed, partly because of the growth of a strong leadership, partly because the New Testament is the greatest book of religion in the world. But in addition to these reasons there was one more—the way in which the Christians lived. They were changed men. The risen Christ was at work among them. Those who formerly had forsaken their wives now lived with them faithfully. Those who had valued riches above all else now shared their goods. Those who had murdered and would not live with men of another tribe now prayed for their enemies. Earnings were placed in a common fund to care for widows, orphans, the aged and the shipwrecked.

"Among us," said one of the early Christians, "you will find uneducated persons, workingmen, old women who are not able to explain in words the good of our teaching, but they show it in deeds. They do not make speeches but do good works. When struck they do not strike again. When robbed they do not go to law. They give to those who ask of them and love their neighbors as themselves."

GROWTH AND STRUGGLE

ROGRESS in the growth of the Church was not stopped by the severe tests. And besides the Christians were not hunted out in all times and not often in all places at once. Persecution in Gaul (now France) did not necessarily mean persecution in Africa or Greece. During the second century, that is, from 100 to 200 after Christ, the blows fell now here now there quite frequently but not everywhere at once. During the third century from 200 to 300 there were two periods of about fifty years each when the Church enjoyed almost complete peace throughout the entire Empire. But at the beginning of the century in 202, and in the middle of 250, and just after the close of the century in 303–304, the emperors tried to crush Christianity throughout the entire Roman world.

Especially in times of peace the Christians gave more definite shape to their ideas. The arguments with the Gnostics raised the question of how to know who was right. The Gnostics claimed to be right because they had in their keeping special teachings of

Jesus, Peter and Paul. The Catholic Christians (the word Catholic means universal) replied by asking to whom Jesus, Peter and Paul would have been most likely to entrust any secret teachings. Would they not have confided such treasures to the bishops whom they selected to take charge of the churches? And among the bishops the favorite would have been the bishop of Rome, for according to the Catholic Church the first bishop in that city was Peter himself, the rock (the word Peter means a rock) on which Christ founded his Church when he said, "Thou art Peter and on this rock I will build my Church. . . . And I will give unto thee the keys of the kingdom of heaven" (Matthew 16: 18, 19). Peter is called the first pope. The word pope comes from a Greek word which means simply father. In the earlier period it was used of any bishop. Later it was given as a title only to the bishop of Rome. On this medal, which is of a later time, the

Pope is shown handing the church to Peter. Protestants are not so sure that he was the first bishop, and in any case think that his power belongs to those who are like him, rather than to those who followed him in office. However that may be, the early Christians in all parts of the world looked to the bishops of Rome as the followers of Peter and as the guardians of any secret teachings handed down from Jesus and the Apostles. If the Christian convert wished the truth let him turn not to the Gnostics but to Rome.

The Gnostics began to write down the supposed secret teach-

ings of our Lord and the apostles in books, and many Christians
set down their different ideas about our religion. Then the
Church was driven to say what books should be accepted and
what should not. There was no New Testament as yet. The
books of the New Testament had been written, but the Church
had not said that these and these only should be received as the
true teaching. Little by little the Catholic Church made up its
mind on the books to take in and the books to leave out of the
canon. The word canon means a ruler by which to keep things
straight, and when a book was taken into the canon it was as if
a mark had been put on the ruler.

First the letters of Paul were accepted and the four gospels
and the book of Acts. The other writings of our New Testament
were slower in finding a place and even John's Gospel had a
struggle. So did the book of Revelation. Hebrews, II Peter,
Jude, James and the second and third letters of John only grad-
ually took their place upon the rule. Not until the fourth
century was the canon closed.

In Christian art the four gospels were indicated by the heavenly creatures seen in a vision by the prophet Ezekiel in the Old
Testament. One creature had the face of a lion, another of an
eagle, another of a calf and the fourth
of a man. These became the symbols of
the Evangelists, as the writers of the
gospels are called. The lion is the sign
of Mark, the eagle of John, the calf of
Luke and the man of Matthew.

The books which were left out of
the canon are called the Apocrypha.
These writings spun stories out of the

imagination to fill up those parts of the life of Jesus and the apostles which are left out or merely hinted at in the New Testament. The Apocrypha tells all about the mother and even the grandmother of Jesus, about his childhood, how he modelled birds in clay and clapping his hands made them fly; how, when a plank in Joseph's carpenter shop was too short, the boy Jesus pulled it out to the right length; how Paul made a trip to Spain and Peter to Rome where he made sardines swim. The Church decided that this sort of thing was neither true nor good enough to find a place in the New Testament.

The Church, then, in the disputes with the Gnostics made the bishops, and especially the bishop of Rome, the source for the unwritten truth and the New Testament the source for the written. The truth itself was set forth in a creed. The word creed comes from the Latin word *credo*, which means "I believe." The Apostles' Creed begins in Latin, *Credo in deum omnipotentem*. These words and the rest of the creed in English are as follows:

I believe in God the Father Almighty,
Maker of heaven and earth, [the Gnostics thought the earth was bad and God the Father did not make it.]
And in Jesus Christ, his only Son, Our Lord,
Who was conceived by the Holy Ghost, [ghost in old English meant spirit.]
Born of the Virgin Mary,
Suffered under Pontius Pilate,
Was crucified, dead and buried. [The Gnostics thought he did not really suffer and die.]
He descended into hell [that is, he visited the spirits who died before he came on earth.]
The third day he rose again from the dead,

He ascended into heaven,
And sitteth on the right hand of God the Father Almighty;
From thence he shall come to judge the quick and the dead. [The
    quick are those who are alive when he comes.]
I believe in the Holy Ghost; [or Holy Spirit.]
The holy Catholic Church; [that is, the Church throughout all the
    world.]
The communion of Saints;
The remission [forgiveness] of sins;
The resurrection of the body, [the early Christians believed our bodies
    would come back to life after death. They would not be just the
    same bodies, however. The Apostle Paul said they would be spiri-
    tual bodies.]
And the life everlasting.

While this creed is called the Apostles' Creed, it was not really by the apostles themselves, but was in very early use in the Church as a confession of faith for those receiving baptism.

The rite of baptism was the initiation of the Christian. It is called a sacrament. This word comes from the Latin *sacramentum*, the vow promised by the soldier. As the soldier swore to serve the emperor so the Christian in baptism promised to serve the King of Kings. Clad in white and bearing lights, the initiates came to the cleansing water. Enough water was preferred for dipping all over, but sprinkling with a few drops was allowed where water was scarce. Baptism was supposed to wash away all earlier sins. Sometimes it was given to babies, but those who had not been baptized as children often preferred to save up the cleansing rite until their deathbeds.

Baptism commonly in the earliest times was out of doors in some running stream. Churches had no baptisteries, that is fonts or bowls for baptism indoors. In fact the churches themselves

were simply rooms in the homes of the Christians. In the long
period of peace real churches began to be built. The oldest Christian church to have been preserved at all was dug up in the
ruins of the city of Dura on the Euphrates river and dates from
the year 232 A.D. The remains of the church have been brought

to the United States and set up in the art museum of Yale University. In the front is a baptistery. On the wall behind it under
the arch are pictures of the Good Shepherd and his sheep and
also of Adam and Eve.

Another sacrament was called the Lord's Supper. The Greek
name for it was Eucharist, which means to give thanks. The
Lord's Supper was a Thanksgiving. At first it was a real meal.
The Apostle Paul complained of the people at Corinth that they
ate and drank too much and advised them to have something
at home before coming. The meal in time was given up and was
replaced by the practice which we have today of using a small

portion of bread and wine. The Christians believed that this bread and wine had a very special meaning. Here is an early prayer to be used at communion:

First for the cup: We thank Thee our Father for the holy vine of David Thy servant which Thou didst make known to us through Jesus, Thy servant. Glory be to Thee forever. And for the broken bread: We thank Thee, our Father, for the life and knowledge which Thou didst make known to us through Jesus, Thy servant. Glory be to Thee forever. As this bread that is broken was scattered as seed upon the mountains and then gathered together and became one, so let Thy Church be gathered together from the ends of the earth into Thy kingdom, for Thine is the glory and the power through Jesus Christ forever.

The terra-cotta lamp shown on this page is decorated with grapes from which came the wine of the Eucharist and with the figure of a fisherman because Jesus told his disciples to be fishers of men.

The services of the early Church were held on Sunday rather than on the Jewish sabbath which lasted from sundown to sundown on Friday and Saturday. The Christians made the change because Sunday is the day when Christ after his death was first seen by his disciples. On this day of the week the Christians who lived in the cities and the country came together. Then the leader read to them from the Old Testament and from the New Testament. After a sermon the congregation rose and prayed. Then bread and wine were brought. The leader gave thanks and all the people said Amen. This is a Hebrew word meaning "So may it be." The word was taken from the language of Jesus without change into Greek or Latin and later into English. Then the deacons served the communion. The first Christians had the Eucharist or Thanksgiving every Sunday.

The preachers talked to the congregations about the great truths of the faith and also about such smaller matters as good manners. Here is an example of Christian instruction from the second century. "Don't cram food into your mouth," said the preacher, "as if you were packing for a journey. Don't talk with food in your mouth and don't try to drink and eat at the same time. Keep laughter in check. Man is not to laugh all the time because he is a laughing animal any more than a horse is to neigh all the time because he is a neighing animal. Too much laughter is called a giggle in women and a guffaw in men. A smile is better, but one need not be gloomy. If attacked by sneezing do not startle the company with the explosion. Women who wear jewelry seem to be afraid that without it they would be mistaken for their servants. Let not women smear their faces with paint. Beauty is the free flower of health. Expensive utensils are not necessary. Won't a knife cut without a jewelled handle? What if a pan be of earthenware? Won't it take the dirt off the hands? Does the table have to have ivory legs to hold a loaf? Won't the lamp give light if made by a potter instead of a goldsmith? Is not a goatskin as good a blanket as a purple quilt? Jesus ate from a common bowl and told his disciples to sit down on the grass. He wiped their feet with a linen towel. He did not bring down a silver footbath from heaven, and he asked the Samaritan woman to give him a drink from an earthenware vessel."

Advice like this was given probably when the Church was at peace. But the peace was broken about every fifty years during the third century. The trial was especially severe in the year 250 after Christ. The Emperor Decius came from the north, from the region around the river Danube, which was only slightly Christianized. He believed that Christianity was weakening the Empire and that to return to the old religion would make Rome great again. In order to stamp out the new religion he required that every one in the Empire should get a certificate from an official, witnessing that the person had sacrificed to the Emperor. Some of these certificates have been preserved in the dry climate of Egypt. One of them reads:

Presented to the commission for the sacrifices in the village of Alexander Island, by Aurelius Diogenes, the son of Satabus, of the village of Alexander Island, about 72 years of age, with a scar on the right eyebrow.

I have at other times always offered to the gods as well as also now in your presence, and according to the rules have offered, sacrificed and eaten of the sacrificial meal; and I pray you to attest this. Farewell. I, Aurelius Diogenes, have presented this. [Then the official wrote] I, Aurelius Syrus, testify as being present that Diogenes sacrificed with us. [Then Diogenes added] First year of the Emperor Cæsar, Gaius, Messus, Quintus, Trajanus Decius, [The emperor had many names. The one by which he is known is Decius], pious, happy, Augustus. 2nd day of Epiphus. [June 25, 250].

Death was the penalty for refusal to obtain a certificate like this.

The Church was caught unawares. During the fifty preceding years of peace strictness had been relaxed. Christians had grown more friendly with the heathen and sometimes had even married with them. Minds were not braced for the trial. Many failed. Some rushed to sacrifice. Bishops even dragged their flocks to the pagan altars. Some Christians went to prison before giving in.

Some endured torture for a time. Others did something which proved very troublesome. They did not sacrifice, but they took these certificates which said that they had. Often the officials were friendly and did not want to kill them. They said to the Christians something like this, "I know you are a Christian. You don't have to sacrifice. Give me some money and I'll let you have a certificate without sacrificing."

And the Christian thought to himself, "The bishop said that we should not sacrifice. I am not going to. The bishop did not say that we could not take certificates. This would not be denying Christ. The official knows I am a Christian. He is going to let me pay a fine for being a Christian instead of cutting off my head. So long as I do not deny Christ why cannot I do this?" The trouble, of course, was that the certificate said the person had sacrificed.

The persecution did not last long and when it was all over many of those who had failed wished to return to the Church. They loved the Lord Jesus in their hearts, and they believed that the Church was like Noah's ark outside of which all life perished. Now these people wanted to get back into the ark.

What should the Church do? Could such offenders be forgiven? Of course God could forgive them, but what of the Church? The answer was that Christ had given to Peter the keys of the kingdom of heaven and what he forgave on earth would be forgiven in heaven. This power had been handed on to those who came after him and particularly to his successor, the bishop of

Rome. The people to be forgiven, of course, must be sorry and must prove their sorrow by coming before the congregation in sackcloth and with ashes on their heads. This is called confession and penance. At first confession was public before the congregation. Later on it became private before the minister or priest.

Some Christians were very angry that the prodigal sons had been forgiven. Such mildness would encourage failure another time and the Church would be made up of weaklings. The strict party went off and started a church of their own which lasted a long time. Three quarters of a century later the Emperor Constantine, who had become a Christian as we shall see, tried to unite this group with the Catholic Church. He asked what was wrong. Was there any difference in belief? There was not. What then was the matter? Just this, was the answer, that the grandchildren of those who were faithful in the trial could not have anything to do with the grandchildren of those who failed. The Emperor in disgust told the bishop of the strict party to set up a ladder and climb to heaven alone.

The persecution of the Emperor Decius was followed by peace again for another half century and then the story repeated itself when the Emperor Diocletian began to persecute. He tried to destroy the churches and all the copies of the Bible. Some even of the clergy gave up the Scriptures, and when it was all over wanted to come back. The point was already settled that the laity, that is, the common Christians, could be taken back, but what of the ministers, the clergy? They, too, were forgiven. But this time another denomination of protest was formed in northern Africa, called the Donatist. To it flocked all the poor and discontented people in the land, some of them very unruly characters who began to tear down the churches and throw acid in the eyes of the bishops of the other party. Even after the whole Roman Empire had become Christian the Donatists were so troublesome that the penalty of death was decreed against them.

Many failed, but not all. If some denied who were expected to confess, some confessed who were expected to deny. A play was given before the Emperor Diocletian in mockery of the Christians. One of the actors was clothed in white in order to be baptized, "I feel so heavy," he cried, and lay down on the stage as if ill. "I want to be made light."

"How are we to do it?" asked his companion. "Shall we shave you like carpenters?"

"Idiots. I want to be a Christian and fly up to God."

Then they sent for a sham minister, who began to use some of the Christian words. Now it happened that the actor when a little boy had been brought up in a Christian home away off in Gaul (France). When these words were said in sport and all the people were laughing he remembered his father and mother and what they had taught him as a lad and he shouted out, "I want to receive the grace of Christ. I want to be born again." The people laughed louder, but the actor said to the Emperor, "Illustrious Emperor and all you people who have laughed loudly, believe me Christ is Lord." When Diocletian learned that he meant it, he caused him to be tortured. His sides were torn with claws and burned with torches, but he kept on saying, "There is no king but Christ whom I have seen and worship. For him I will die a thousand times. I am sorry for my sin and for becoming so late a soldier of the true King."

ROME TAKES THE CROSS

ONSTANTINE put a stop to the persecution of the Christians. He was the Emperor after Diocletian, but he did not become Emperor until after a long struggle, nor was he a Christian at first. Diocletian had thought the Empire was too large for one man to manage and for that reason parcelled different sections out to assistant emperors. When he grew old and retired, the assistant emperors began to quarrel and the sons of the assistant emperors began to quarrel too. Constantine was the son of one, Maxentius was the son of another. Constantine held Britain (England) and Gaul (France). Maxentius held Rome and Italy. As Constantine marched toward Rome he is said to have seen at sunset a cross of light above the sun with these words *Hoc Signo Vinces* which mean, "By this sign thou shalt conquer." At any rate the Church was now so powerful in the Empire that Constantine believed the Christian God must be a very powerful God. This God he would serve in the hope of victory, and victory was his. The troops of Maxentius

32

retreated too hurriedly onto pontoon bridges across the Tiber river. The bridges broke. Maxentius himself was drowned. This is called the Battle of the Milvian Bridge and happened in the year 312 A.D. Constantine had won Italy. He had to struggle for over ten years to overcome other rivals and become the only Emperor. Wherever he ruled persecution stopped, and when he was completely victorious Christianity became the most favored religion of the Empire. Jesus of Nazareth, crucified at the command of a Roman governor, had come to be worshipped as the Savior of the Roman Empire.

The coins of the period show the change. Some of the coins of the pagan empire had been stamped with the picture of the wolf and the twins, Romulus and Remus. The new coins added the monogram of Christ. The wolf had become a Christian. On another coin the Goddess of Rome appeared holding in her hand a globe bearing the same monogram. Rome had become Christian. On another Mithras, the sun god, held a globe with a star on one side and the cross on the other. Mithras had become Christian.

The monogram appeared also on the battle standard of Constantine's army. One may wonder how this might be since the early Christians had refused to be soldiers. The an-

swer is that ideas had changed. Since Constantine promised if he won to protect the Christians, they could not help wishing him to win and some were willing to help him win. When at last all enemies were conquered the Christians hailed Constantine as a deliverer sent by God.

He did much for the Church directly and indirectly. Directly he gave to Christian ministers the privileges formerly enjoyed by pagan priests. Churches were to have the same rights as pagan temples. The Christian Sunday was made a legal holiday. Christian bishops were held in high honor and were permitted to travel like senators in government coaches. Churches destroyed in the persecution were rebuilt at the expense of the pagans and Constantine himself built a number of new churches including Sancta Sophia [Holy Wisdom] at Constantinople.

Churches were called basilikas. Here is the ground plan of the Basilika of Saint Peter's at Rome. C is the apse where sat the bishop and the clergy behind the communion table, which came

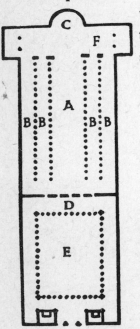

to be known as the altar because in the Jewish temple the animals were sacrificed upon the great stone altar as offerings to God. So upon the Christian table the body and blood of Christ in the form of bread and wine were offered up to the Father. F is the transept and extends out a little on the sides suggesting the form of a cross. A is the nave. This was for the choir. The people were in the aisles marked B. The women were on one side and the men on the other. At communion they came up from opposite sides. The next picture, which is supposedly of the Last Supper, really shows how the people at a later time came from opposite sides to the altar. D is a covered court called a narthex and E an open court called an atrium. In these courts according to the weather were gathered the catechumens, that is, Christian beginners not yet far enough along in their religion to be admitted to communion and to the church itself. Basilikas came to be very

beautiful. Saint Jerome complained: "Basilikas are built at state expense. The roofs are adorned with gold and interlaid with marble. The holy books of the Christians which once were given to the flames are now bound in purple and inlaid with gold and jewels."

Constantine helped the Church indirectly by changing the capital of the Empire from Rome to Constantinople. This city was better situated for ruling the whole Empire because it lay on the intersection of the lines connecting Europe and Asia by land and the Ægæan Sea and the Black Sea by water. The city had previously been called Byzantium. Constantine named it after himself, Constantinople, which name the Turks have turned into Istanbul. It was also called New Rome. Old Rome ceased to be the capital. There was no Emperor there. In consequence the pope of Rome came to be regarded as in a certain sense the suc-

cessor of the Emperor and legend said that Constantine granted the rulership of the western part of the Empire to Silvester I, the bishop of Rome. Though the story is not true it contains a truth. The Church was beginning to grow up into the place of the Empire.

Constantine had chosen Christianity not so much because of the vision of the cross, if indeed he ever saw it, but because the Empire needed a religion to hold all of its different peoples together. Christianity, which had spread so rapidly and grown so powerful, appeared to be the best religion to serve as a cement for the Roman world. What was Constantine's dismay when he found the cement beginning to crack!

A quarrel broke out among the Christians themselves about the relations of Christ, God and the Holy Spirit. All Christians were

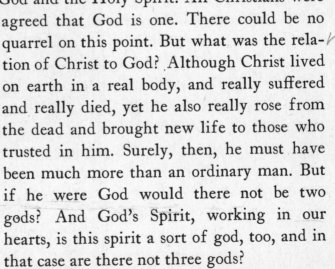

agreed that God is one. There could be no quarrel on this point. But what was the relation of Christ to God? Although Christ lived on earth in a real body, and really suffered and really died, yet he also really rose from the dead and brought new life to those who trusted in him. Surely, then, he must have been much more than an ordinary man. But if he were God would there not be two gods? And God's Spirit, working in our hearts, is this spirit a sort of god, too, and in that case are there not three gods?

The dispute became heated in the city of Alexandria where an aged priest named Arius claimed that Christ was indeed more than man, but less than God. A young dea-

con in the same Church, Athanasius by name—he became bishop
and is shown in the previous picture in his bishop's robes—
Athanasius said that the views of Arius would never do. If Christ
were more than man and less than God he would be neither one
nor the other. Athanasius said that there is one God. Christ shared
in the being of God. We all do in a measure. Christ shared completely and helps us to share more fully. The Spirit shares completely too. God is one. But within the One are three, sharing in
his being, the Father who is the Lord of all the universe, the Son
who lived on earth and for us died and rose, and the Spirit who
breathes upon our spirits and teaches us the things of God.

The three who thus share in the being of God are called the
Trinity. At a later time the Church worked out their relations in
this diagram. The Trinity is
shown with one head and
three faces. The winged creatures in the corners stand for
Matthew, Mark, Luke and
John. The diagram is too simple to describe the mystery of
God and pictures like this
were frowned upon by the
leaders of the Church, but
the common people liked
them.

In the dispute over the relations of Christ and the
Father the love of Christ was
forgotten. Discussion ended
in riots. Constantine was

shocked that Christians should quarrel at all. He understood very little about the debate itself and sent a messenger to rebuke both parties. "The whole dispute," said he, "is the result of a quarrelsome spirit among people who haven't enough to do. Because of a foolish difference in words should brethren treat each other as enemies?"

This advice did no good. There were other disputes too. Easter was being observed in different places at different times. Some followed the spring full moon like the Jews at Passover. Some kept the first day of spring when the heathen celebrated the rising of the gods of nature. In this case the day of the week varied. Others insisted that Easter must always be on Sunday, the day on which Christ first appeared risen from the dead.

To settle all these questions Constantine called a council at the city of Nicæa near Constantinople in the year 325 after Christ. This meeting is known as the Nicene Council and was the first gathering of the leaders of the whole Church. From all the world the bishops came, from Africa and Syria, from Mesopotamia and Persia, Pontus, Galatia, Pamphylia, Cilicia and Phrygia, from Thrace, Macedonia and Achaia and from far distant Spain. Priests came from Rome. Never, said the historian of the gathering, had a prince gathered such a garland in honor of his Savior as had Constantine.

The bishops and priests assembled in a great hall and waited for the Emperor. At his approach all rose. He seemed like a heavenly messenger clothed with raiment glittering as with rays of light, brilliant with the splendor of gold and precious stones. The Emperor invited all the members to dinner. As they marched into the dining hall, on each side stood soldiers of the imperial bodyguard with swords drawn—no longer to punish but to honor the

Christians. Among the bishops was one whose eye had been gouged out in the persecution. Constantine kissed the place where it had been.

The Nicene Council settled that Easter should fall, as it does now, on the first Sunday after the first full moon, after the vernal equinox, which is the first day of spring. Thus the Jewish, pagan and Christian practices were combined.

The dispute as to the relationship of Christ and God was settled according to the views of Athanasius. The creed now called the Nicene Creed was not drawn up until some years later, but it deserves the name Nicene, because it really has the ideas of the Nicene Council. The words in the translation of the English Book of Common Prayer are these:

I believe in one God the Father Almighty,
Maker of heaven and earth,
And of all things visible and invisible:
And in one Lord Jesus Christ,
The only-begotten Son of God,
Begotten of his Father before all worlds:
God of God, Light of Light,
Very God of very God,
Begotten not made,
Being of one substance [or being] with the Father,
By whom all things were made;
Who, for us men, and for our salvation,
Came down from heaven,

And was incarnate by the Holy Ghost of the Virgin Mary,
   [came to live in human flesh through the Spirit of God]
And was made man,
And was crucified also for us under Pontius Pilate.
He suffered, and was buried;

And the third day he rose again according to the Scriptures;
And ascended into heaven,
And sitteth on the right hand of the Father.
And he shall come again with glory
To judge both the quick and the dead;
Whose kingdom shall have no end.

And I believe in the Holy Ghost,
The Lord and Giver of Life,
Who proceedeth from the Father and the Son,
[God's Spirit comes to us directly from God, but also through Christ]
Who with the Father and the Son together is worshipped and glorified;
Who spake by the Prophets,
[God's Spirit was speaking through the prophets of the Old Testament]
And I believe one Catholic and Apostolic Church.
I acknowledge one Baptism for the remission of sins:
And I look for the Resurrection of the dead;
And the Life of the world to come. Amen.

The members of the council then presented the results of their work to Constantine. They are shown doing so in the picture at the end of this chapter. Five members, including the aged Arius, refused to sign and were banished.

This by no means solved all the difficulties. The discussion about the relation of Christ to the Father and of the divine and human elements in Christ himself went on and on over a period of many years. The banished bishops came back and Athanasius in turn was exiled. Then Constantine died and was followed by his three sons. They fought for the throne and the beliefs of the Arian and Nicene groups became all tangled up in their disputes. The victorious side would banish the bishops of the other party. Even the aged messenger whom Constantine had sent

to Alexandria to stop the quarrel was himself banished. He protested to one of the sons of Constantine, "I was persecuted under
your grandfather" (that is, the father of Constantine who had
been one of the assistant emperors under Diocletian), he wrote,
"and if you are going to persecute me I will bear it rather than
deny the truth, but remember that God has given to you the
Empire and to us the Church. If we steal the government we
oppose God, and if you meddle with the Church you do wrong."

The day was to come when the Nicene party won out completely. Then a law of the Roman Empire was passed that any one
who did not believe in the Trinity should be put to death. This law
was later to be used against the Unitarians.

THE FLIGHT TO THE DESERT

IF, when the world becomes Christian, church-men become as lordly as senators, and emperors banish bishops, what should the serious Christian do? "Get out of the world," answered some. "Go to the desert. Flee the world, flee the cities. Go back to the fields where the farmer sings psalms at the plough. Flee the murderous emperors and the sleek minis-ters. Flee everybody and live all alone." The people who did this were called hermits and monks. Hermit means one who lives in the desert. Monk means one who lives alone. The first monks were hermits. But later hermit was used of one who lived entirely alone, and monk of one who left the world of cities and families to live apart with a group of other monks. The movement began in Egypt.

The hermits and monks believed that the world was bad and also that the body was bad. Here they were falling into the ideas of the Gnostics. If the body is bad, then, said they, it must be beaten down by hardship. For this reason they lived in caves and

42

slept on rocks, and ate only enough to keep alive, often just dates and cabbages. Some went without sleep till they were so drowsy that at meals the food would fall from their mouths. Contests arose as to who could stand the most hardship. One monk stood on a single leg like a stork until he fainted. Others lived on the tops of high pillars and had their food sent up on poles.

The first monks were so strict that they would not even look at women. This picture shows a monk being visited by his mother and some of her friends. He has to keep his hand over his eyes during the entire talk, though he looks as if he were peeping.

Living alone in this fashion without friends and work is not good for people. The hermits with no one to talk to and little to do imagined that devils were after them. Saint Anthony spent most of the time fighting the devils in his mind. Artists have had a grand time drawing his devils. The following picture is from "The Temptations of Saint Anthony" by a French artist, Jacques Callot. The hermits soon found out that living entirely

alone drives one crazy, so they decided to live in communities known as monasteries. But they did not live in families. The men had monasteries and the women had nunneries.

Even though they had

withdrawn from the world, the monks did not feel quite right about going off and leaving it. The world was still there and all the people in it. The monks could not help wondering what was going on. An old legend tells how one day a man from the world went to visit a hermit on the top of a mountain. The hermit said, "How are things getting on in the world? Do people have enough faith so that they could say to this mountain, 'Rise up and be cast into the sea'?" As these words were spoken the mountain on which the hermit and his visitor were sitting rose right up. "Oh, mountain," said the monk, "I was not giving orders. I was just reciting the Bible. Sit down." And the mountain sat down. This story shows at least that the monk was thinking about the world.

And when the world was in trouble the monks did come back. In times of famine they returned and persuaded the rich to share their food with the poor. Another story tells that a monk of Alexandria in Egypt often came into the city. He knew a rich young woman who was very greedy and to her he went and said, "I know how to get you a set of jewels at a very low price. If you give me five hundred pieces of silver I can get them for you." She entrusted him with the money but he never brought the jewels. She asked the reason. "I'll show you the jewels," answered the monk, "and if you are not satisfied you may have your money back." Then he took the young woman to a house.

"Would you like to see first the emeralds or the gems?"

"It doesn't matter."

He took her first to his hospital for lepers. "There are my emeralds." Next he showed the cripples. "These are my gems. Will you have your money back?"

"No, it's worth it."

One of the great monks was Saint Jerome. He began as a hermit but the desert did not help his thoughts. He was alone save for the beasts, yet dreamed of dancing girls in Rome. Though he beat his chest with a rock his thoughts still troubled him. After some years he gave up and came back to the world of men. A lion followed him and, if one may trust the pictures, was sure to go wherever he went.

Jerome became a great student. He learned Hebrew and trans-

lated the Old Testament from that language into Latin and the New Testament from Greek into Latin. The translation of Saint Jerome is called the Vulgate. It is the Bible of the Catholic Church. For the people who cannot read Latin an English translation has been prepared.

Saint Jerome was not so strict as the first monks had been about having absolutely nothing to do with women. His monastery was at Bethlehem. Some noble women of Rome came and established a nunnery nearby. They helped him with his translation. One of them had a married sister at Rome to whom a baby girl had just been born. Jerome wrote to the mother, "Send the baby to her aunt at Bethlehem. Let her grow up near the manger of the Savior. She won't learn to lie here. She will live like an angel. Or send her to me. I will teach her myself. [The monks did teach children.] I will take her in my arms. I will help her with her first lispings, old man that I am." (He was over sixty.) The baby never came. The barbarians were thundering down the roads to Rome. The Eternal City fell, and soon the refugees were pouring into the monastery at Bethlehem. Jerome had his hands full looking after them.

Another great monk was Chrysostom. As a young man he desired to join the brothers on the hills above Antioch in Syria, but his widowed mother held him back. "Your father died as soon as you were born," she reminded her son, "and you do not know how hard it was for me to take care of you. I knew nothing about business and taxes, the rascality of servants and the meanness of relatives eager to get my money. But I went through all this for you and I was happy. Don't think I want to make you unhappy, but I do want you to stay with me till I die." Chrysostom stayed.

When she died he became a monk, but little by little he came to feel that the more heroic life is that of the bishop who helps people just as they are in the world. His is a more difficult task than the monk's. A bishop has to instruct his flock. He must care for strangers. He must look after the women, scold them when they are idle, soothe them when they are in trouble. He must be a good mixer with all kinds of men. He must settle the quarrels of his congregation, argue with the Arians and preach to people used to the excitement of the racetrack. Again the bishop must give communion to the worthy and refuse it to the unworthy and live with them afterwards. All this is more difficult than sleeping on a rough bed and going without a bath. Chrysostom was soon to choose the more heroic life of the bishop of Antioch.

The members of his congregation had forgotten the generosity of the days of the Apostles. Chrysostom sought to revive that spirit. "Recall," said he, "that money is like water. It goes bad if it does not run. Don't think you have done enough because you beat down your body with fasting. I don't object to your fasting, but helping others is more important. And don't ask for lovely things if they are made by blood. Recall: a ship has to be fitted and rowers enlisted, a man for the prow and a helmsman. A sail is spread and an ocean covered. Wife and children are left behind. The merchant entrusts himself to the waves and goes to the lands of the barbarians and undergoes innumerable dangers. And for what? In order that you may have colored threads to weave into your slippers.

"Better use your money for the poor. How many are there in Antioch? I should say fifty thousand. And how many Christians? I should say a hundred thousand and the rest Jews and pagans. Now if the Christians were to bring in goods and share them like the Apostles, couldn't we take care of the poor, especially if we did it as they do in the monasteries? There all the cooking for the whole group is done at once and that is much cheaper. Let us learn from the monasteries. Who ever starved there?" The monastery was thus beginning to teach the world.

And the monk was able to give good advice to the married. "A wife should never say to her husband, 'You lazy good-for-nothing sluggard. Look at that man over there. He has come up from nothing. There's something to him. He takes risks and makes voyages. He has made a fortune, and his wife wears jewels and goes out with a pair of milk-white mules.'

"If she does talk like this her husband should say, 'I could have married another wife with a better fortune and of a noble family, but I picked you because I loved you. You are so beautiful and modest and gentle.' Then he shall talk to her of true wisdom with some words on the foolishness of riches.'"

Chrysostom had some hard things to say, but people let him because they knew him and loved him. His fame as a preacher went over all the Empire. The name Chrysostom means the Golden Mouthed. His real name was John.

The patriarchate at Constantinople happened to become vacant. Patriarch was the title of the bishops of the more important cities. Constantinople was the most important after Rome. A patriarch was needed at Constantinople. Chrysostom's fame was great. The Emperor's prime minister wanted him for the post, but well knew that Chrysostom loved Antioch and Antioch loved him, and would never let him go. Chrysostom was kidnapped and carried to Constantinople and made patriarch.

That was a sorry day for him. The people at Constantinople did not know him and when he preached there as he had done at Antioch against the rich, they grew angry. When he criticized  fancy dresses, the women and the Empress were enraged. Here she is shown in all her finery on a coin. And when Chrysostom tried to reform the clergy they were surly. The patriarch of Alexandria in Egypt was cross because he had wanted the place at Constantinople for himself. All of these people combined together to put Chrysostom out. He was banished and died in exile. The Church in Constantinople always had a hard time. The Emperor was too near and insisted on ruling the Church. The Pope at Rome had an easier time because the Emperor was farther away.

During the days of Chrysostom Christmas was placed, as it is now, on December 25, and he helped to make the change. Before his time it had been on January 6. The reason for the change was that the pagans in the Empire observed on December 25 the birth-day of the sungod Mithras, because on their calendar the 25th (on ours it is the 21st) was the shortest day of the year when the sun started on his upward course again. On this day was a big celebration, and the Christians so enjoyed it that they would join their pagan friends and fall away from the Church. For that reason the bishops decided to have a Christian feast on the same day and moved Christmas so that the birth of Christ would displace the birth of Mithras.

The first picture of the baby Jesus in the manger comes from this time. In it the Wise Men appear twice: on the left as they first espy the star and on the right as they bring their gifts.

CHAPTER
SIX

As Rome Fell

HE Church in the west in the meantime was being sorely tried because of the barbarians pushing into the Empire. To catch up with the story there we must go back to a time before the fall of Rome, when the Romans were trying to protect the frontiers. Rome itself was so far away from the boundary that the government was moved up to Milan in upper Italy. The officer in charge of this region was Ambrose. He had been brought up in a Christian family, but had never been baptized. The bishop of Milan died and a new one had to be chosen. There was great excitement because the Arian quarrel had not yet died out and both the Nicene and Arian parties wanted to put in their man. Ambrose feared a riot and came to the church to keep the peace. As he walked in, a child called out, "Ambrose for bishop." And all the people cried, "Ambrose for bishop." Nothing that he could say would stop them. He had not even been baptized, but they took care of that. He was run through baptism and all the lower grades of the clergy and made a bishop in a week.

50

He had never been a monk like Saint Jerome and Saint Chrysostom, but he admired the monks and after he became a bishop spent much time with them. He had all the courage of a Chrysostom in standing against rulers who interfered with the Church or did wrong and he was more successful, perhaps because he had been trained as an official of the government rather than as a monk.

His first great quarrel was with the Empress Justina, who belonged to the Arian party. Ambrose was of the Nicene party. The Empress wanted one basilika for the Arians in Milan. Ambrose refused to give them any at all. His reason was not simply that he considered the Arian position wrong, but that Arianism had come to be the religion of the Goths, who had been converted by missionaries from the Roman Empire at the time when the Arian party was on top. In the years following most of the Empire accepted the Nicene view while the Arian faith spread among the barbarians with the result that Arian had come to mean barbarian and Nicene Roman. The Empress was hiring barbarian soldiers to defend the Empire against other barbarians. Here is a picture of one of them as shown in their own crude drawing. For these soldiers of the Arian faith she desired a church in Milan.

Ambrose refused and with his followers filled up the church which she desired. The Empress sent barbarian troops to surround the church. Ambrose, while waiting to see what the soldiers would do, taught his people to sing some of the hymns which he had written. He is called the father of hymn singing in the

Latin language. The Empress had not the heart to command an attack on a congregation of singers. Ambrose won.

A more important conflict happened with the Emperor Theodosius. He was a great general and very successful in keeping back the barbarians. There was no trouble with him over Arianism. But there was something else. He had a hot temper. At Thessalonika (Saloniki today) there was a famous chariot driver. He was guilty of a crime for which he had been arrested by an officer of the Emperor. The games came. The people wanted the driver and killed the officer. "Very well," said the Emperor Theodosius. "They shall have their games." Into the great amphitheatre thronged seven thousand people. The soldiers went in too. The entrances were closed and the seven thousand were all killed.

Shortly afterwards the Emperor came to Milan and to the church of Saint Ambrose for communion. The bishop met him at the door. "You cannot enter here with hands soiled by human blood." The Emperor had to promise never to carry out a sentence of death until forty days afterwards lest anything be done in anger and he had to do penance before being admitted to communion. Chrysostom in the east had not been able to defy the Empress. Ambrose succeeded in the west with Empress and Emperor alike. This was a sign of the way things were to work out in the east and the west. In the east the Emperor was to rule the Church; in the west popes were to command kings.

That day, however, was a long way off. The Roman Empire itself had first to pass away in the west. At a time when the old world was breaking up and the new had not yet come, lived a man whose thinking did much to shape the world which he did not live to see. He is called Saint Augustine of Hippo, a little town in northern Africa. We know more about him than about most men of his time because he wrote the story of his own life, and he told what had gone on inside him as no one before had ever told.

As a lad, he relates, he belonged to a gang of boys who played until late one night and then made a raid on a neighbor's pear tree which was laden with fruit, but tempting neither in color nor in taste because the pears were not ripe. "We took huge loads," says Augustine, "but we did not eat them, but just nibbled and threw them to the pigs. It was mean, but I loved it. Why did we do it? A murderer does not kill just for killing. He wants to get even or to take something from the man he kills, but we robbed the tree for nothing at all. I am sure of this, that I should never have done it if I had been alone. The gang spirit carried us along. When some one said, 'Let's go. Let's do it,' each was ashamed to come out and say that he would be ashamed to do it. We chuckled to think of the prank we were playing on the owner sound asleep, little suspecting that his tree was being stripped. It was mean. I hate now to think about it."

Augustine's father was a pagan until late in life. His mother, Monica, was a Christian and worried greatly over her son. She hoped he would become a Christian and talked with the bishop about him, who said, "Don't worry. The son of so many tears cannot be lost."

When Augustine grew older he became a father and had to have money to take care of his boy and the boy's mother. For that reason he became a school teacher in Carthage, a city not far from his home. But the boys were unruly as he had been himself. He heard that teaching was easier at Rome and, without telling his mother, slipped off, taking his boy and the boy's mother. Teaching in Rome was easier. The boys were well behaved but skipped off just before pay day. Augustine was glad when a better place opened at Milan. His mother learned that he was there and joined him.

Milan was the city of Saint Ambrose. Augustine went to hear him preach. As a teacher he was interested to see how the preacher used his hands, and his voice and made up his sentences. Augustine soon found something more than graceful hands and smooth words. Here was a man who knew the power of God. Here was a brave man, a decisive man. Augustine wished he could be like that. Whenever he had been in a tight place he had always run away. If he could be like Ambrose! But Augustine was not ready to change yet.

He was not married to the mother of his boy. His own mother wanted him to send her back to Africa and that he should marry some one else. To please his mother he did send her back and then took some one else without getting married either. At this point in his life he heard the story of the monks in Egypt who lived away from women altogether. He was astonished that these simple men could make themselves live such hard lives. And there was Ambrose who acted like a monk even though a bishop.

Full of worry, Augustine went off by himself into a garden and beat his breast and tore his hair. "Queer," he thought, "that when I tell my hand to beat my breast and tear my hair it does it, but when I tell my mind to do something, it won't." Then Augustine heard the voice of a child playing in a house near by. The child was repeating, "Take up and read. Take up and read." He went over to a seat and found there a copy of the New Testament. As he took it up, the pages opened at the words in Paul's letter to the Romans, "Not in rioting and drunkenness . . . but put on the Lord Jesus and do not follow the desires of the flesh.

Augustine surrendered. "I bowed my neck to the yoke that is easy and my shoulders to the burden that is light, Lord Jesus, my strength and my Redeemer." And he went and told his mother. With his son he was baptized a little later by Ambrose of Milan.

Then the party started back for Africa. Monica fell sick on the way and died. Augustine was at first too overcome even to cry. He sang the hymns of Ambrose and his tears were unstopped. With his son he returned to Africa and then the boy died. Alone now, Augustine became a monk and wanted to spend his days in peace, but he was called to be the bishop of Hippo. The picture on preceding page shows him with his bishop's hat on the table. As a matter of fact he did not have a hat like that. The picture was done later and shows the kind of hat used in the Middle Ages. The rod, like a shepherd's crook, is called a crozier. It is the sign of a bishop. This too was not used until later.

A hard time it was to be a bishop! The barbarians were sweeping over the Empire. Why did God let them? Some thought he was angry with the Arians. That was Ambrose's explanation. But why then did the Nicene party suffer too? Saint Augustine sought a deeper answer. The fight which is going on now, he said, is only a part of a fight which is always going on, not only on earth but in heaven between the forces of good and evil. These forces break out on earth and a Cain kills an Abel. The Roman Empire, for the most part, was like Cain and grew by taking land from other peoples. It was the result of the greed of men. The barbarians are only paying Rome back for what she did to others. The Roman Empire will pass. Something else will come, is already beginning now. The Christian Church, although it is not perfect, is an expression of the forces making for good. We need not be troubled too much if Rome passes away, provided the Church remains. Augustine did not mean that the Church should take the place of the Roman Empire. He wanted to have a government as well as a Church, but the government should be guided by the Church. The popes later tried to fulfill his dream.

Yet nothing on earth lasts, nothing except love. Saint Augustine has an interesting comparison of love and money. "Money," he said, "is made smaller if you give it away, but love grows. We show more kindness to a man when we give him money if we do not ask it back, but we do not give love unless we require it to be repaid. When money is received it stays with him who receives it and leaves him who gives it, but love does not leave the man who gives it and if it is not repaid, still it stays with him, and he who receives it does not possess it unless he gives it back."

Saint Augustine is great in his preaching. He is greater in his prayers. "Late have I loved Thee whose fairness is so old and yet so new. Late have I loved Thee. And behold Thou wert within and I without and there I sought Thee. Unlovely I broke upon the loveliness which Thou hadst fashioned. Thou wert with me and I was not with Thee. Long was I held from Thee by those things which without Thee are naught. Thou didst call and cry and burst my deafness. Thou didst gleam and glow and dispel my blindness. Thou didst exhale fragrance. I drew breath and I pant after Thee. I have tasted and do hunger and thirst. Thou hast touched me and I burned for Thy peace. Thou hast made us for Thyself and our hearts are restless till they find their rest in Thee."

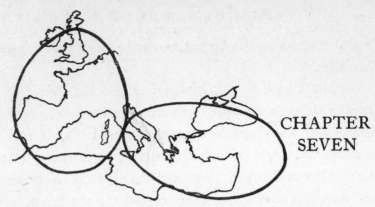

THE CHURCHES OF THE EAST

ARTITION of the Roman Empire in which Christianity had its beginnings resulted from the inroads of barbarian peoples from the north. Rome had been in the center of that older world. After the invasions it was to be rather on the edge of two worlds, the western and the eastern Roman Empires. Each had something the shape of an egg. The eastern portion still called itself the Roman Empire and the people long spoke of themselves as Romans though as a matter of fact their language was Greek. Latin was spoken in the west. For a time after the old Roman Empire broke up the Church held together, but in the course of the centuries the division of the Empire split the Church into a Latin branch and a Greek branch. The Latin part is called the Catholic Church and the Greek the Orthodox, which means the Church with the right teaching. Later there came to be more than one Catholic Church and more than one Orthodox Church. We have today the Roman Catholic and the English or Anglo-

Catholic and also the Greek Orthodox and the Russian Orthodox Churches.

We shall look in this chapter at the Churches of the Eastern Empire. Constantinople was the capital and, as we have said, Greek was the language; yet not entirely. There were other peoples besides the Greeks in this Eastern Empire. The Armenians, the Syrians and the Ethiopians had their own languages and did not like the Greeks, nor their Empire, nor their Church, and for that reason formed separate Churches of their own.

These unhappy quarrels had one fortunate result in that Christianity was able thereby to spread into Persia. The Persians were fighting with the Greek Empire and would not accept any religion in favor among the Greeks, but when the Empire drove out some of the Syrian Christians, known as Nestorians, they were welcome in Persia and were able to convert many of the people. Later some of the Nestorians pushed on into China. When the World War of 1914 drove the Nestorians from their ancient homes in Persia a number came to New York.

The Greek Emperors made many attempts to win back the separated Churches and also to conquer the barbarians in the west and recover Rome. The most successful was the great Emperor Justinian in the sixth century who for a brief period regained much of the old Roman Empire. His reign is best remembered for two things, both of which had to do with the Church.

The first was the rebuilding of the beautiful church of Sancta Sophia which to this day stands in Constantinople. The first church of Sancta Sophia had been built by Constantine. In Justinian's time the structure burned down. Within forty days after the fire Justinian started to rebuild. Ten thousand workmen were employed and paid daily in fine silver. The Emperor appeared before them in his royal robes and encouraged them by his presence. As a result of these enormous labors the church was rebuilt in five years, eleven months and ten days from the laying of the first stone and was dedicated on Christmas day of the year 537. The style used for the church was not that of the basilika. Instead of the oblong shape a central dome was used with smaller domes around it. This kind of architecture is called Byzantine from Byzantium, the old name of Constantinople. The slender

spires on the sides in the picture are called minarets and were added later by the Mohammedans when they captured the city and turned the church into a mosque. The Turks recently have made it into a museum.

The other great achievement of the Emperor Justinian was the gathering up and sorting out of the laws of the Roman Empire into one system called the Code of Justinian. Parts of this law had to do with the Christian religion and the Church. The code says that any who refuse to believe in the Trinity and any who repeat baptism shall be put to death. The first was aimed at the Arians, the second at the Donatists, those unruly folk in northern Africa who had broken away from the Catholic Church and become so troublesome after the persecution of Diocletian. Not even a Christian government could put up with their violence, but unhappily the law by which they were punished was aimed not at their conduct but at their belief. In as much as they considered themselves to be the only true Church they would not accept the baptism of those who had been baptized by the Catholics and later joined the Donatists. In such instances baptism was repeated. The law of the Roman Empire made this the offense, and the same law centuries after was used against the Baptists.

After Justinian the parts of the Roman Empire recovered in the west were lost again and much of the east was lost too because of another inroad which came from Arabia. The sign of the new invaders was the crescent moon and their cry was, "There is one God, Allah, and Mohammed is his prophet." These were the Mohammedans. Their prophet had attacked the worship of idols and taught instead the worship of the one God. Allah is his name. He is the same as the god of the Jews and of the Christians. Mohammed might perhaps have become a Jew or a Christian if he had known these religions at their best. But the only Christians he had known were people like the Gnostics. He was willing to say that Moses and Jesus were prophets, but Mohammed himself was *the* prophet.

He taught his followers to break the idols and never to make any pictures or carvings in human form in the mosques, which are the Mohammedan churches. Mohammedans are expected to pray five times a day turning their faces to Mecca where stands the holy shrine of their faith. Mohammed encouraged his followers to fight for Allah who would reward them in a heaven flowing with rivers of cold water, milk, honey and wine. On earth, however, they were not to drink wine. The teaching of Mohammed is set forth in a book called the Koran. The warriors of Allah compelled conquered peoples either to accept the Koran or pay taxes or be killed.

The movement of conquest started in 622 A.D., and spread all the more quickly because the Armenians, Syrians and Ethiopians were being oppressed by the Greek Emperor and were glad to come under the rule of the Mohammedans who did not disturb the religion of the conquered provided taxes were paid. The hosts of Allah swept over Palestine, Egypt, northern Africa and Spain up to the gates of France. Here they were stopped, just a hundred years after the movement began. Oddly enough the lands taken

by the Mohammedans had roughly the form of a crescent which in the course of the years shifted backwards. (See p. 68.) One tip moved from the lower edge of France to the lower edge of Spain and the other tip moved across Constantinople up to the gates of Vienna. The Eastern Roman Empire became smaller and smaller until conquered entirely by the Turks in 1453.

The Mohammedan invasion affected Christianity in other ways

than by reducing territory. The Mohammedan example of allowing no images of the divine in human shape may have been the reason why some Christians began to object to the many religious images with which the churches had come to be filled. The plain cross without any body had been replaced by the crucifix with the body of Christ fully carved upon the cross. The Virgin Mary, called the Mother of God, had many images. The Greek name for image is *icon*. Some of the saints likewise had icons. A saint means one who is very good. There are official saints who because they were very good have been given the title of saint by the Church, such as Saint Paul, Saint Peter, Saint Jerome, Saint Augustine. Because the saints were so good their prayers are supposed to have more weight with God. The saints, though no longer on earth, are believed to be alive in heaven and were supposed to pray for those who honored their icons. A saint who looks out for particular persons or countries is called a patron saint. Saint Christopher is the patron of travellers. The patron saint of England is Saint George and of Russia is Saint Andrew. The common people in the Greek Empire kissed the icons, put them down dry wells to bring the water back and trusted them to do other feats of magic.

The Emperor Leo, called the Isaurian, wished to stop these crude practices, and therefore ordered his soldiers to hew down a crucifix on the gate of Constantinople. When the soldiers climbed a ladder and began to hack, a mob of women pulled the ladder from under them and caused their deaths. A great quarrel started called the Iconoclastic Controversy. The word iconoclast comes from the Greek word for image and another word meaning to break. The women and the monks loved the images and compared the Iconoclasts to the Roman soldiers who crucified Christ. In the pictures below, on one side a soldier is giving Christ the sponge of vinegar and in the other picture the Iconoclasts are doing the same thing to the image of Christ. A bishop in favor of the images defended them in this way: "They are the books of the unlearned," said he. "The man

who cannot read sees the image and his mind is lifted up from the image to that for which it stands." A council at Nicæa in 781 restored the images. This was the last council at which the Greek and Roman Churches agreed.

Iconoclasm left this lasting effect that in the Eastern Churches fully rounded sculpture was given up and bas-relief was used instead because this flat sculpture is more like a plain picture and less like a pagan idol. The Greek and Russian icons will hang flat on the wall. The Roman Catholic Church, however, allows fully rounded statues of Our Lord and Lady and of the saints.

This was not the only difference between the Roman and Greek

Churches. They had been drifting apart for a long time. The real trouble was that the old Roman Empire had broken up. Greek, once spoken in Rome, was being forgotten. The marvel is that the Churches did not separate sooner. In spite of differences they held together until the year 1054 A.D.

The points which were given as the reason for the separation were not very important, though they are still objects of difference between the Catholic and Orthodox  Churches. The Catholic clergy are generally clean shaven. The Eastern clergy have long beards. At the time of the separation the rule was going through in the West that none of the clergy could be married. The Eastern Churches allow the clergy up to the rank of bishop to have wives. Another point has to do with belief. Both Churches agree that the Holy Spirit of God comes to us from God. But the Catholics point out that the Spirit of God does not come to those who are not Christians as much as to those who are. Consequently they say that the Spirit of God comes from the Father and from the Son. The Greeks refuse to accept the words "And from the Son."

From the Greek Church Christianity spread among the Slavic peoples such as the Serbs, Bulgarians and Russians. These people at one time all spoke the same language. Into that language the service of the Church was translated. After separate languages developed in different Slavic countries the Church service continued the same for them all. The liturgy or form of worship has thus helped to keep the Slavic peoples together.

Russia became Christian under Vladimir I in the year 988 A.D. His grandmother Olga had been a Christian but without converting her people. Legend says that Vladimir was in doubt what religion to accept for his country. There were many religions and the Christian religion was by that time practically divided into two branches, the Roman Catholic and the Greek Orthodox. The chronicler says that messengers of the various religions and Churches came to the court of Vladimir to present their claims. First the Mohammedan painted the joys of paradise. Vladimir was quite pleased until he learned that he would not be able to drink wine on earth. "That would never do," said he. "Drinking is the joy of the Russians." Then the Jew spoke, but Vladimir said he could not accept the religion of a people without a country. The Roman Catholic was dismissed because Vladimir's grandmother, Olga, had not received her religion from Rome. The Greek painted a terrible picture of the last Judgment and of all the torments to be endured by those who failed to accept the Orthodox Faith.

Vladimir decided to look into the Greek religion further and sent some of his men to Constantinople. They were taken to the church of Sancta Sophia. The magnificence of the buildings, the throng of the clergy, the gorgeous vestments, the enchanting strains of the choir, the sweet odor of the incense, the procession of the deacons carrying torches—all so enthralled the messengers that when they made their report Vladimir's immediate word was, "Where shall we be baptized?"

The Russian Church for many years was a daughter of the Greek Church. But when the eastern Roman Empire fell to the

Turks the Russians said that as Constantinople had been the second Rome, so Moscow should be the third. The Czar was made the head of the Russian Orthodox Church. The architecture of the Russian Church buildings is noted for its many spiral domes called "onion" domes."

By the twentieth century the Russian Church had come to be very wealthy and many, though certainly not all, of the priests were lazy and worthless. The Bolshevik revolutionists hated the Church because of its wealth and when they came into power many churches were plundered and many priests were killed. But Christianity is not dead in Russia and the faithful still gather at Easter to celebrate the rising of their Lord.

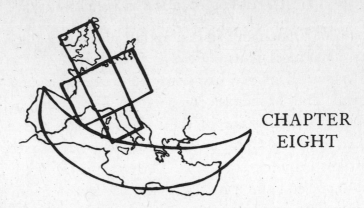

TAMING THE BARBARIANS

RESH waves of barbarian invasions brought the Roman Empire to an end in the west. Various people from the north, some Arian Christians, some pagans swept in and set up independent kingdoms in what are now the separate nations of Europe. The Vandals reached northern Africa; the Suevi and the Visigoths were in Spain—later they were in turn overcome by the Mohammedans—Goths and Franks were in France; Goths and Lombards in Italy; Angles and Saxons in England. Some of these names are still used. The name France comes from the Franks. Upper Italy is still called Lombardy, and England is short for Angleland. The invaders were far from killing all the people in the Roman Empire. Sometimes the former owners became servants on what had been their own lands, and sometimes part of the land was taken away from them and they were allowed to keep the rest. In time the older and the newer peoples intermarried and became one. South of the Rhine River the language of Rome lived on in somewhat altered form.

Spanish, French and Italian are all much like Latin, and English has taken most of its big words from Latin.

When all of the invasions were over the map had changed again. The Mohammedans, as we have seen, held a territory roughly in the shape of their emblem, the crescent. The lands taken by the northern invaders curiously had also the shape of the Christian emblem, the cross. The upright ran from Italy through Scotland, and the arms from the border of Spain up into Germany. Those arms were to extend and the Crescent was pushed back.

The task of teaching these northern peoples in the ways of Rome and in the ways of Christ fell to the Church. The Roman Catholic Church became the successor in a way of the Roman Empire and the popes of Rome carried on much of the power and influence of the emperors. In the great task of winning the west the popes were immensely helped by the monks. The first monks were so disgusted with what happened to Christianity after the world became Christian that they fled to the desert to get away from the world entirely. But when the world was in such difficulties the monks of the west undertook to help make a new world. This they did in two ways. First by building monasteries in safe places such as mountain tops and the islands of the sea where the old Romans could get away from the roughness of the barbarians; secondly, by planting among the barbarians themselves monasteries from which the light of Christianity could shine in the surrounding darkness.

We shall look at the first great pope of the new west. His name was Gregory I. He is called Gregory the Great. He became pope in the year 590 A.D. shortly after the time of the Emperor Justinian. The gains of that Emperor in the west had been lost and the barbarians were again in control of much of Italy. The government at Constantinople was unable to handle the intruders and the government at Rome almost as powerless. The only one who could do anything was the Pope and he had the power because he had the money. How the Church came to have so much money we cannot trace in detail. We do know that people had long been  giving lands to the Church. The record has come down to us of one farmer who willed his lands and his pigs to the Church for the forgiveness of his sins. There must have been many people with many sins, for the Church had come to own many pigs and many lands, eighteen hundred square miles in all and luckily most of it in southern Italy or on the islands which the barbarians did not hold at that time. From these lands the Church had an income of about a million and a half dollars a year.

The Pope had to manage the farming of these lands. Clerks looked after the accounts. Slaves did the manual labor. The slaves had been given with the land. The Church did not free them, but tried to treat them well. Pope Gregory spent the money sometimes for the Church. Baptismal robes were sent to converted Jews, blankets to the monks of Sinai, and timber for a church in Egypt. The report came back that the logs were too short. "Sorry," wrote Gregory, "the ship was too short. When a longer one sails I will send you longer logs." Sometimes the Pope sent gifts to individual poor folk. To one he wrote, "I am sending you a duck and a duckling that whenever you see them you may think of me."

But Gregory also spent his money for the sort of thing which before had been done by the government. The food for the people of Rome had been supplied by the government. Now the Pope owned the grain lands and the ships. Also when the Romans were captured by the barbarians the Pope paid the ransom. He was the only one who had enough money. He also made treaties with the barbarian Lombards. In all this he was acting practically as the ruler of the country. He took to himself these tasks not because he wanted to, but because nobody else was able to. The Church saw a need and stepped in to meet it.

The Pope had dealings with the countries round about, with the Emperor at Constantinople, with the barbarian kingdoms in Spain, France and England. We shall look at them in a moment.

In all of these efforts on behalf of the Church and the people the Pope was greatly aided by the monks. He had been a monk himself and would have been glad to spend his days in a monastery. The man who changed monasticism to meet the needs of the new world of the west was Saint Benedict. He lived in Italy. When the barbarians were disturbing the country he provided a place of safety for refugees by building his monastery high on a mountain cliff. The place is called Monte Cassino.

The rule of Saint Benedict became the charter of western monasticism. Some of the points of the rule were old, as that the monks should be unmarried, poor and obedient. There was a new rule that they should stay at home. The hermit monks had sometimes made a nuisance of themselves by wandering like tramps. The monks of Saint Benedict could not leave without special permission. For that reason the monastery had to provide everything necessary for life; fields and rivers, a well, a bakery and a kitchen. The monks had to do all of their own work of farming, cutting

down trees, cooking and serving. The day was divided among hand-work, prayer and meditation by oneself, songs and readings together, study, meals and sleep. The rising bell was at two in the morning, but this was not so bad because bed was at six. The divisions of the day varied with the seasons. Here is a sample: from 2:00 to 4:00 prayer; 4:00–4:15 meditation; 4:15–6:00 prayer; 6:00–9:00 study; 9:00–12:00 work in the fields; dinner at noon. The hour of noon used to be at 3:00 in the afternoon. Noon comes from a Latin word *nona* which means the ninth hour. Counting from 6:00 that would be 3:00 in the afternoon. The monks were required to wait until "noon" for dinner. They could not change the rule, but they did move up the hour. That is why noon is now at 12:00. The monks ate in perfect silence while one of their number, who had already eaten, read to them from some good book. If a monk desired anything at the table he was directed to ask for it by signs as, for example, for an apple "put thy thumb in thy fist, and close thy hand and move afore thee to and fro"; for milk, "draw thy left little finger in the manner of milking"; for mustard, "hold thy nose in the upper part of thy right fist, and rub it"; for salt, "flip with thy right thumb and thy forefinger over the left thumb." After dinner came naps;

then work again in the fields; at sundown evensong and bed, with the young monks sandwiched between the old to prevent any scuffle.

The monks had no possessions of their own but were supplied with beds and blankets, upper and under garments. Each monk had a knife, a needle and a stylus for writing. Knives were not to be kept under pillows lest some one get hurt if there were a tussle. The food would seem plain to us. Not often did they have four and twenty black-birds, but of rough fare they had enough. No one starved. The cooking and serving were done by the brothers in turn. At the beginning of the week the one on kitchen duty prayed that he would make no mistakes and at the end of the week cleaned up the ones he had made. A special

table was served for the guests and the abbot ate with them. He was the father of the monastery. The word abbot comes from the Hebrew word *abba* meaning father. The rule says, "The abbot must not be worried nor anxious neither should he be too demanding or stubborn or jealous or over-suspicious, for then he will never be at rest." The monks were to obey him in every-thing, but he was to consult them even to the youngest, and all were to confess to each other their faults.

The monasteries were intended partly as retreats from a troubled world where men might live quietly and win their way to heaven. But they were more than retreats. Visitors might come and receive the best of entertainment. The monks served the world, too, in

other ways, by their prayers and by their hands. The monasteries
by and by were built no longer on safe islands or mountain tops but
right in the midst of the barbarians whom the monks taught how
to break the land and build roads and bridges. The monks also took

children and taught school and copied books. All of this had to be
done by hand before the days of printing. The monks gave the
most loving care to their work and made letters with colored inks
of exquisite loveliness. The first letter of the page often had a
picture inside. This was called an illuminated initial. Some of them
in black and white have been used at the beginnings of the chapters
in this book. Here are two of the letter Q showing the monks
occupied in log splitting and in harvesting.

CHAPTER
NINE

THE WINNING OF THE NORTH

GREAT task lay before the popes and the monks in the conversion of the west. The barbarians who came into the Empire were already mostly Christianized, though they had been won only for the Arian and not for the Nicene faith. The ideas which separated these two parties had been largely forgotten, but the difference was still important because the Arian Christians did not recognize the leadership of the Pope. Other barbarians were pagans. They were all warlike folk, who were attracted to Christianity chiefly because it was the religion of the mighty Roman Empire and they supposed that to become as mighty as Rome they would have to become Christian.

Some parts of Christianity seemed to them very strange. They were a fighting people and had no use for the teachings of Jesus about meekness and turning the other cheek when struck. Their hero was the Apostle Peter because when his Master was attacked in the garden of Gethsemane he wielded his mighty sword and cut off the High Priest's servant's ear. Neither could they understand why any one should refrain from marriage or should wish to leave the world. The monk appeared to them if not as crazy then certainly as altogether too good for this life.

These were the people whom the Church had to win. There were also some pagans who might be called old barbarians instead of new. Some of them had once been within the Roman Empire. None of them were invaders. The Celts were a people who lived in northern France and the British Isles. Those in France and England had been converted in Roman days, but not those in Ireland and Scotland. The Angles and Saxons were new barbarians who pushed the Celts into Wales. The Welsh were then the only Christians left in the British Isles. All the rest had to be won for Christ.

The popes and monks undertook the task, and for the rest of Europe as well. We shall look at the winning of one country after another. First comes Ireland. The patron saint of that country is Saint Patrick. He did more than any other to win the island for the Christian faith. His work for the Irish was a case of returning good for evil, for they had made him a slave. At the time when the Roman legions were being called home from England to defend Rome, Patrick was living somewhere near the border of Wales. The Irish swooped down on the English coast and carried him off. He was set to herd swine.

Patrick had been brought up as a Christian. His father was a deacon. But the lad had never cared much for his religion when at home. Now that trouble came upon him he prayed that he might find a way of escape, and the chance came. He succeeded in reaching the seacoast and managed to obtain a ride on a boat by offering to take care of the cargo of dogs being shipped to France.

Once in that country he went to a monastery, one of those built for safety on an island of the Mediterranean Sea. Here he might have stayed, but he was eager to see his family again and after many hardships reached home once more.

Gladly would he have remained had he not had a dream one night in which the babies of Ireland pleaded with him to come back to their country and teach them about Christ. Patrick decided to return, but first he must learn more about Christianity. For that reason he went to France and studied for a number of years in a monastery. At length he was sent out with the approval of the Pope to be a missionary to the people among whom he had once been a slave.

Of his work among them we know little because only legends have come down to us. One is that a certain king sent messengers to give Patrick a bronze cauldron. When they returned the king asked, "What did he say?"

"*Grazacham,*" they answered. This was short for the Latin *gratiam agimus,* and means thank you.

"Was that all he said?" asked the king. "Then go and take it away from him."

They did and returned. "What did he say this time?"

"*Grazacham.*"

"What? Thank you for giving and thank you for taking away. Then give it back to him and give him some land besides."

Two points in this story are true. One is that Patrick spoke Latin and taught the Irish the language of Rome. The army of the Roman Empire never reached the island. The customs of Rome were brought by the missionary. Later on Ireland was to send back many learned men to teach the people of Europe.

The other point is that the king gave Patrick land. All life among the barbarian peoples was built around land. They had no large cities. They lived on the land and the way in which they showed thanks to the Church was by giving land. On the land the Church planted the cross. Here is an Irish cross. The interlacing ribbon design is common on the Irish manuscripts.

Another story of Patrick is that he went back one day to the mountain where as a slave he had herded swine. On the top of the mountain he sat and thought of the strange ways of God who had let him be made a slave in order that he might learn to know and love this people and come back to them with the story of Jesus. As Patrick mused he felt gathering about him the spirits of those who before him had worked for Christ, and the spirits of those who should come after. Alone, he was not lonely.

And they did come. Ireland became Christian and from Ireland missionaries went to other parts. They went over to Scotland. Columba founded a monastery on the island of Iona from which as a base the monks converted Scotland. From Scotland they began to work down into England. There, as we recall, the pagan Angles and Saxons had broken in and pushed the Christian Britons into Wales. While the missionaries from Scotland were working down from the north other missionaries sent by the Pope landed in the south and worked up.

This brings us back to Pope Gregory. He was the one who sent the missionaries to the south of England. The legend is that he became interested in the English because one day in the market place at Rome he saw some English boys for sale as slaves.

"Who are they?" he asked.

"Angles," was the reply.

To which Gregory, who had had no experience with English boys, responded, "Not Angles, but angels."

At any rate the Pope sent Saint Augustine as a missionary to England. He is called Augustine of Canterbury to distinguish him from Augustine of Hippo.

King Ethelbert of Kent, whose wife Bertha was already a Christian, received the missionaries, but only out of doors for fear of the magic which they might work indoors. Well might the king be afraid if the report were true that Saint Augustine could make tails grow on the backs of those who irritated him. Really he did have magic—magic of a different sort, the magic of a new hope. When a pagan king in England asked his advisers what they thought of the Christian faith, one of them replied, "Oh King, the life of man is like the flight of a swallow through our banquet hall, out of the dark and the cold for a moment through the light and warmth and into the cold and dark again. A religion which can tell us more about that dark beyond certainly ought to be followed."

While the missionaries from Rome were working up from the south the missionaries from Scotland were working down from the north into England. By and by they met and found out that in the time of separation differences had grown up between the Irish-Scotch practices and the Roman. One difference was as to the manner of the haircuts of the monks. As far back as the days of Saint Jerome the monks had commenced shaving their heads because they were then easier to keep clean in lands where water was scarce. The shaving of the head is called a tonsure. Not quite the whole head was shaved and a difference had arisen as to just which part to shave and which to leave. The Irish shaved from the ears up and left a little tuft on top like a halo. The Roman monks shaved on the top and left a little rim around the ears like a crown of thorns.

Another dispute had to do with the date of Easter. All accepted the practice decided on at the Council of Nicæa that Easter should fall on the first Sunday after the first full moon after the vernal equinox. But to figure out on this basis just when Easter will be for ten years in advance is no light task. The Irish were following

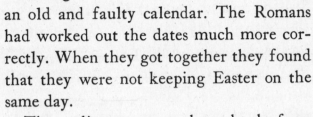

an old and faulty calendar. The Romans had worked out the dates much more correctly. When they got together they found that they were not keeping Easter on the same day.

These disputes were brought before King Oswy who did not know what to say until he was told that the Roman missionaries came from the church of Saint Peter to whom Christ gave the keys of the kingdom of heaven. The king was afraid of being out of favor with the doorkeeper of heaven and decided in favor of Rome.

In England the work of the first missionaries was carried on by churchmen and rulers. One great need was to turn the Bible and other books into the Saxon language which is the basis of the English tongue. The work was begun according to the legend by the earliest English poet Cædmon, a herdsman, who, being downcast because he could not sing like others to the harp, went to bed and dreamed that he was told to sing the story of crea-

tion. In his dream he began to make up verses and when he woke
told them to his master who took him to a monastery. As the story
of the Bible was told to him he turned it promptly into Saxon
verse. Much of this verse has come down to us in a manuscript
very quaintly illustrated, as in this drawing of Abraham enter-
taining the angel. Both Abraham and the angel are dressed as
Saxons. Just how much of the verse was really written by Cædmon
himself is hard to tell.

King Alfred, the Saxon, who ruled over a portion of England in
the ninth century, felt that as the Greeks turned the Hebrew Bible
into their tongue and as the Latins turned both Hebrew and Greek
into their own language so now all three should be carried over
into English. He him-
self, with the aid of
learned bishops, trans-
lated the rule for the
clergy of Pope Gregory
the Great into the Saxon
tongue. The most fa-
mous churchman of the
Saxon period was Dun-
stan, the Archbishop
(which means the chief
bishop) of Canterbury.

He tried to improve the lives of the clergy and founded many
monasteries. Legend says that he pinched the devil's nose with a
pair of pliers. The devil in this picture, as in many others of the
Middle Ages, is shown with an extra face. Whether the saint
pinched the other nose the legend does not state.

But we must come back to the other countries to be won for the faith. France had been converted before the barbarians broke in. Most of the country was Christian even by the time of Constantine. One of the missionaries who helped to finish the first conversion of France was Saint Martin. While a soldier and not yet a Christian he met one day a man in next to nothing. Martin had

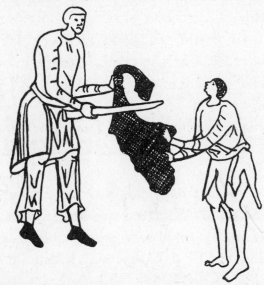

only one garment himself (this picture gives him a bit too much), but he cut it in two and gave half to the beggar. That night in a dream Martin saw the half he had given away on Christ himself. Martin then became a Christian and left the army to become a monk. Later he was made a bishop. Through him many pagans were won for the faith. The most extraordinary stories are told of the cures worked by Saint Martin both alive and dead. His body was supposed to have such power that when the remains were moved from one province to another some beggars fearing that if it came too close their sores would be cured and they would be able to beg no more, started running for the border, but they were too slow and their sores got well.

The work of Saint Martin was not entirely undone when the barbarians broke in, because, as we have seen, they did not kill off all the people in the Empire, but settled among them and in time came to accept their religion. The Franks were pagans. They came over to the Christian faith under their king, Clovis. He was married to Clotilde, a Christian princess, who tried to win him for her Lord. Clovis would not listen, until one day in battle he was in danger of defeat. Then he cried, "Jesus Christ whom Clotilde calls the Son of the Living God, help me and I vow that if I win I will be baptized in Thy name. My gods are not helping me and plainly have no power. Now I call on Thee. Only save me from my enemies." Clovis won and was baptized with all his host.

The conversion of Germany was due largely to a missionary who came from England. Winifred was his English name but he is commonly known by his Latin name, Boniface. He began among a tribe called the Frisians, but was driven out by them and then worked farther up the Rhine. The Germans had a great oak sacred to their god Wotan. Boniface said he would cut it down and prove that Wotan was no god. The people came together expecting to see Boniface struck down, but when the axe smote the tree legend relates that a great gust of sudden wind rent the trunk into four parts which Boniface split into planks for a church. In order to instruct the people who accepted Christianity Boniface really did build a monastery at Fulda. Before his death four hundred monks were working there.

Boniface was now seventy-five. He had never forgiven himself for his first failure among the Frisians. Back he went and had such success that the pagans were angered and came upon him and his companions with swords. His followers would have defended him but he said, "Do not fight, for we are bidden to return good for evil. Be brave and have no fear of those who can kill only the body." The pagans smote them all and then hunted for treasure, but could find only manuscripts and relics.

The northern Germans, called Saxons—some of them had gone into England—were forced to the faith by a king of the Franks called Charlemagne at whom we shall look in the next chapter. He fought the Saxons for twenty-six years until at last they agreed to give in and accept his rule and his faith. We can well imagine that they would learn little of the real nature of Christianity when it was handed to them on the point of a sword as in the picture below. Happily some Christians objected to such methods. A Saxon scholar at the court of Charlemagne, named Alcuin, said, "If as much trouble were taken to preach the easy yoke of Christ to the stubborn Saxons as to squeeze money out of them perhaps they would not stand out so strongly against baptism. Missionaries ought to be preachers and not plunderers."

Fortunately such rough methods were not often used and most of the peoples of Europe were won for the faith in gentler and more Christian ways. Ansgar, the missionary to the Danes, relied on better means. He trusted neither in force nor in magic and when praised for his miracles he answered, "The greatest miracle will be if God ever makes me a good man." That miracle happened and many were taken captive by the sermon of his life.

CHAPTER TEN

KINGS HELP AND HINDER

OLIDIFYING the old Romans and the new barbarians was in great measure the work of the Church. A marriage was made between the strong rough folk of the north and the refined people of the south, and the Church brought about the union. The popes sent missionaries and monks to all the northern regions, bringing to them one faith and one tongue, the Latin language, which came to be understood by educated people all over Europe.

The Church, however, was not the only body making for the unity of Europe. The State also helped. Popes, missionaries and monks were assisted by kings and emperors. Conditions were not as they had been in the old Roman Empire where there had been only one state. The barbarians had many kingdoms much smaller than the present nations, and often at war. But the minds of men could not rest in a world of fragments. The Roman Empire had been one. The new world taking shape in the west must also be one, a new Roman Empire. As the Greeks believed that Rome had passed over to Constantinople, so the Franks thought that the Empire of Rome was to live again among them, and one of their kings founded the Holy Roman Empire, which for centuries bound together in a loose way the many little kingdoms of Europe. Not all of Europe, however, was ever included. England never was, and France only for a time. When, then, we speak of the State in the Middle Ages we are not thinking of a single government, but of many little units and one large one, which served at least in men's minds to unite the world.

The Church and the State for a time helped each other. The State was glad to have the Church teach the people the same faith and the same language that they might the better understand each other and work together. The kings also looked to the Church for their crowns, since many kings were just strong men who ruled because they were strong enough to rule. Yet they found rulership hard if it rested on nothing but strength. The people would not long obey a king unless he were set to rule over them by God and how could men be made more sure of God's approval of a ruler than if the Church gave him the crown? This was the way in which kings had been chosen and anointed in the Old Testament. The prophet Samuel had anointed Saul and later chose and anointed David. In the same way the popes should anoint and crown kings. Pippin, the King of the Franks, received his crown from the Church. His son Charlemagne was made Holy Roman Emperor by the Church. His real name was simply Charles. He was called Charles the Great, which in Latin is *Carolus Magnus*. These are the words around his head on the medal at the beginning of this chapter. In French the words became Charlemagne. He went to Rome and on Christmas Day of the year 800 A.D. was praying in the church of Saint Peter (the front of this church is shown on this coin of Charlemagne). As he was kneeling before the tomb of the saint the Pope slipped up from behind and placed a crown upon his head, hailing him as the Holy Roman Emperor.

In return the kings and the emperors helped the Church. Even the Pope had troubles with the bar-
barians in Italy. Pippin came down
and took five cities away from them
and turned the keys of the cities over to
the Pope that he should be henceforth
their ruler. This was the beginning of
the Papacy as a kingdom. From 754
A.D. to 1870 the popes themselves
ruled over a goodly part of Italy.

At first Church and State helped each other, but as each grew more powerful disputes arose between them. Such quarrels are hard to avoid even though both Church and State claim to be Christian and holy. The trouble is that Church and State overlap. The State deals with man's outward life on earth, with order, justice and peace. The Church deals with man's inner life and his preparation for heaven; with conscience, reverence and the heart of man. One way to divide the work of State and Church would be to let the first look after the body and life on earth, and to let the second look after the soul and the way to heaven. But the division is not so simple. The soul is not out of the body, and the way to heaven cannot be found off the earth. The matter is doubly hard when the Church is itself a government and the owner of many lands on earth. When both Church and State under-
take to rule the life of man, disputes are almost certain to come.

Conflicts of Church and State in the Middle Ages occurred when the Church interfered with the State by refusing to let kings do as they liked about marriages. They would often make matches for themselves or their children in order to cement the friendship of the country with a neighboring state through a marriage of a prince of the one with a princess of the other, or the reverse. The bride and groom might never have seen each other until they were married. Sometimes they liked each other after the wedding and sometimes they did not and wished to be divorced. Then, too, the interests of the country might change and a marriage with some other prince or princess might seem more desirable. The Catholic Church in such cases would permit no divorce because marriage is as much a sacrament as baptism and the Lord's Supper. When people are married they promise to be faithful to each other "so long as they both shall live."

If a quarrel between a husband and wife did occur the Church tried first to bring them together again as this monk is doing. If these efforts failed and the king would not stay with his wife, the Church had two weapons with which to punish him. The first was excommunication. This meant that the king would not be

permitted to come to communion, that is, to the Lord's Supper, nor could he have any other of the comforts of the Church. Another weapon was the interdict. This was an excommunication which applied to the king's territory. If he were the king of France then all the services of the Church would stop in the whole of France. The king's subjects would then be so annoyed that they would try to make the king obey the pope. The "walking interdict" was somewhat milder and applied only to the land within so many miles of the king's person. If he travelled he carried the interdict with him, and every one desired that he move on.

A case happened in France when King Philip was married to a Swedish princess, Ingeborg, without having seen her in advance. When he first set eyes on her he said a shiver went down his spine. After the marriage he put her away. The Pope, in consequence, applied the interdict to France. The people hated it, and when the King surrendered by taking his wife back, and the interdict was removed, the rejoicing was so great that three hundred people were crushed in the celebration.

Other quarrels arose because the State interfered with the Church. The reason was that the Church owned as much as half the land in France and Germany. The possession of the land by the Church had at first seemed desirable even to the State. When the Christian monks went to the northern barbarians the simplest way for the monks to live was to take a tract of unused land and farm it. In the course of time, however, immense stretches of land were given to the Church, and difficulties arose with the State because all taxes came from the land and soldiers for the army were furnished by the holders of land from their helpers. Naturally, then, the King wished the land to be in the hands of those who would pay the money and give the men. The King, therefore, began to appoint the bishops and abbots himself. To this the Pope objected, and whenever the King asked too much of the bishops and abbots they appealed to the Pope and he backed them up. The question, then, was whether the bishop and abbot were servants of the Pope or of the King.

The quarrel applied also to the choice of the Pope because the King or Emperor, to make sure that the Pope would not interfere with the choice of the bishops, insisted on choosing the Pope himself. To prevent this the popes made the rule that the Pope should

be chosen by the cardinals. They are churchmen who live in Rome and help the Pope. They wear flat red hats. The Pope wears a three-layer crown called a tiara.

With the question of lands and loyalty went another as to whether the clergy should be married. They were married especially in Germany. The married bishops had sons and handed on to them the lands of the Church. The Pope believed that the bishops would be more obedient to him if chosen always by him instead of following their fathers. The way to bring this about would be to require that the clergy be celibate, which means unmarried.

The attempt of the Church to make the bishops loyal only to the Pope and to make them give up their wives caused a great fight with the Holy Roman Emperor and with the German bishops who sided with him against the Pope because they were unwilling to give up their wives. The Pope who fought the battle was Gregory VII. The Emperor was Henry IV.

This Pope came out with two orders. All the bishops in Germany must receive the staff of office from the Pope and not from the Emperor, and all the bishops of Germany must give up their wives. They replied that they would rather give up their lives and the Emperor defied the order by appointing a bishop himself in Milan, the old city of Saint Ambrose. The Pope promptly, in the name of Saint Peter, put the Emperor out of the Church and released all Christians from their promises to obey him.

Henry found that he could not be Emperor. The common people would not obey. The only hope was to make peace with the Church. Henry started for Rome. The year was already far along, and the swift Rhine was frozen over. In December, Henry and a little party crossed the Alps. The feet of the horses were tied together and they were dragged down the snow slopes. Not many reached the plain alive. The Pope in the meantime had started north for a meeting and had reached the fortress of Canossa in northern Italy. Henry turned in here and came to the gate of the castle. It was January now of the year 1077. Snow was still on the ground. Henry, clad in white as a penitent and with bare feet, stood all day before the castle. The gate did not open. The second day he stood barefoot in the snow. The gate did not open. The third day he stood again in vain. Yet the successor of Peter could scarcely refuse to forgive one who stood at the door and knocked. The gate opened. The mighty Emperor stood a suppliant before the bandy-legged little Pope, asked forgiveness and made many promises. The Pope forgave.

But the tables were soon turned. The Emperor, once more in control of the country, forgot his promises and then the Pope excommunicated him again. But the Emperor persuaded the people that this time the Pope had gone too far. The Emperor marched on Rome, drove out the Pope and set up some one else in his stead. In the end another Pope and another Emperor came to an agreement that the bishops must be pleasing and loyal both to the Pope and to the Emperor. And the bishops had to give up their wives. From that day forward the priests of the Roman Catholic Church have been unmarried.

Another point on which Church and State quarrelled was as to the courts. The Church had courts of its own. The Apostle Paul had said that Christians should not go to the law courts. For that reason the practice grew up of letting the bishop settle disputes among Christians and a body of law called the Canon Law was formed to guide the bishops. But the State continued to have courts and when the Church and the State were working together the question could not be avoided as to which courts should handle what. By common consent the Church took care of the cases of widows and orphans not of age and of all marriage cases. The dispute with the State arose because the Church demanded that all clergymen including even those who sang in the choir should be tried only in the Church courts no matter what they had done. The King argued that if they had committed crimes they should be tried like any one else in the courts of the State.

The quarrel came to a head in England where King Henry II had forced on the Church the choice of his old chum Thomas à Becket as the Archbishop of Canterbury. The King supposed that Thomas would do his will, but in this he missed his man, for the gay courtier, once he was made a bishop, became a stout champion of the Church. The King in hot anger exclaimed before his men, "A fellow who has eaten my bread has lifted up his heel against me. He first came to my court on a lame horse and now he acts as if he were the King. Will none of the cowards who eat my bread rid me of this bothersome priest?" Four knights who overheard these words went off and murdered the Archbishop in his cathedral. So great was the horror through- out England that the King had to allow himself to be whipped at the tomb of Saint Thomas.

Pilgrimages became com- mon to the martyr's grave. The pilgrims on their way enter- tained each other with stories, which the poet Geoffrey Chaucer gathered together in verse in the *Canterbury Tales*. To this day the stones of the floor of Canterbury Cathedral are worn in front of the spot where the people once kneeled before the martyr's shrine.

The greatest success of the Church in its dealings with the Empire and the various states of Europe came in the thirteenth century under the great Pope Innocent III. He was more nearly the master of Europe than any king or emperor. With no army, but only the power of his word as the successor of Saint Peter, and with the weapons of excommunication and interdict he gave kingdoms and took them away. Here is a picture of a pope giving 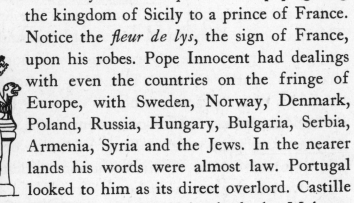 the kingdom of Sicily to a prince of France. Notice the *fleur de lys*, the sign of France, upon his robes. Pope Innocent had dealings with even the countries on the fringe of Europe, with Sweden, Norway, Denmark, Poland, Russia, Hungary, Bulgaria, Serbia, Armenia, Syria and the Jews. In the nearer lands his words were almost law. Portugal looked to him as its direct overlord. Castille and Aragon at his command united to drive back the Mohammedans in Spain. In France King Philip took back his wife Ingeborg, as we have seen.

In England King John appointed his own man as the Archbishop of Canterbury. The Pope insisted instead on the election of Stephen Langton, one of the noblest of Englishmen. King John swore by the teeth of God that he would put out all the eyes and cut off all the noses of all the Italians in England and drive out all the bishops and the monks rather than accept the Pope's man. The Pope put England under an interdict. The King had to give in and promise that England would be subject to the Pope and pay him a goodly sum of money every year.

The Church had many faults and many failures, but in spite of them all she was the greatest force for justice and order in the world of the Middle Ages.

CHAPTER ELEVEN

Mighty Deeds

ACCOMPLISHMENTS of a high order are to the credit of the Church in the Middle Ages. She was the greatest force in the lives of men. To them she gave courage and hope and tried to guide their feet in the way of life. The Church was neither perfectly good, nor perfectly wise, but no other society tried so hard or did so much.

The Church tried to keep the peace. The nobles were continually fighting with each other, wasting each other's lands, destroying each other's castles and carrying off each other's servants. Such practices were hard to stop. The Church tried at least to limit them. The Peace of God required that warfare at any time should be kept within certain bounds. There should be no attacks on the buildings of the Church, nor upon clergymen, pilgrims, merchants, women, and farmers; and cattle and farming tools should be spared. The plan did not work any too well. The Church made another attempt and sought to stop all warfare for part of the time. This plan was called the Truce of God. All fighting should cease from Saturday noon to Monday morning and entirely at certain seasons of the year such as Advent (the month before Christmas) and Lent (the forty days before Easter). Neither did this plan work very well.

The Pope then tried another way. If Christians would fight, let them not fight each other, but let them rather go against the enemies of the faith. Let them attack the Turks, a rough people who had recently adopted the faith of Mohammed and had broken into the Holy Land, where Jesus lived and died. The pilgrims who travelled to see the sacred places were maltreated by the Turks. Pope Urban, himself a Frenchman, went to the town of Claremont in France and there called the nobles before him. In stirring words he painted for them the terror of the Turks. "An accursed race," he said, "has invaded the lands of the East. Christians are enslaved, tortured, killed. The swordsmen practice on them to see whether a neck can be cut in two with one blow. Churches are used as stables, or wrecked or turned into Mohammedan mosques. The Church of the Blessed Virgin Mary is in their hands. Who can take vengeance if not you who have won glory in arms? But you are swollen with pride and cut each other to pieces. Come now to the defense of Christ. Forget feuds, fight infidels. Before you is the standard bearer, leading you to his war, the unseen standard bearer, even Christ."

And all the host shouted, "God wills it. God wills it."

The crusade had begun. The word crusade comes from a word meaning cross, because the crusaders sewed upon their sleeves a cross in colored cloth. That winter the preparations were made. Under the blows of the blacksmiths' hammers the hot iron clanged and took shape as shields and swords, stirrups and armor. The hosts gathered from different parts, and by different roads and seas crossed to the East. In the year 1099 Jerusalem was taken. The infidels were slaughtered and the crusaders rejoiced in the Church of the Holy Sepulchre where Christ was supposed to have been buried.

But the Holy Land was easier to take than to hold. The Turks made fresh inroads. New crusades were sent against them. One of the best known is that of Richard the Lion Hearted. But no crusade was long successful. When three had failed a boy in France named Stephen believed that Christ appeared to him and promised that what the grownups had been unable to do the children should accomplish. Let them trust not in their swords and their strong right arms but in the Lord of Hosts who would work miracles for them and cause the sea to roll back that they might pass on dry earth like Moses and the children of Israel when they walked through the Red Sea dry shod on their way to the promised land. Stephen took his stand at the spot where pilgrims thronged and called to the children of France to join the new crusade. They came. By thousands they came. Their mothers and fathers

could not hold them back. The news reached Germany and another boy named Nicholas issued the same call and to him also the children came. By thousands they came, a great host, mostly of boys about twelve, some girls.

The German children started first, marching up the Rhine and singing as they journeyed through the pleasant land:

> Fair are the meadows,
> Fairer still the woodlands,
>   Robed in the blooming garb of spring;
> Jesus is fairer, Jesus is purer,
>   Who makes the woeful heart to sing.

The way at first was not too hard. The valley of the Rhine had towns and villages where food could be obtained. But when the children left the river to march through the forests of Switzerland the country was not so well settled. Food was then hard to get. Robbers and wild beasts lurked in the woods and fell upon any who strayed from the host in search of nourishment. At length the crests of the Alps loomed ahead. At the sight of the craggy cliffs some turned back. Others pressed forward only to leave their bones upon the Alpine snows. Some thousands, however, made the climb in safety and came down upon the plains of northern Italy over which they marched to the sea. But the sea did not roll back for them. Broken hearted, a number stopped right there and grew up to be Italians. The rest trudged on to Rome for the blessing of the Holy Father. And he blessed them, but told them to go home until they were older to fulfill their crusader's vows.

The children under Stephen marched through France to the city of Marseilles on the coast, and for them also the sea did not open. But a way even better offered itself. Some kindly merchants placed their ships at the service of the children. Here is a picture of small crusading vessels. Seven ships the merchants had and each held seven hundred men. Hence there must have been about five thousand chil-

dren. They boarded the ships and were never heard of again for eighteen years. Then a new crusade set out, of grown men this time, no doubt some of those children whom the Pope had advised to grow up first. They reached Egypt and there

found a survivor of the children's crusade who told them what had happened. Two vessels were driven by a storm upon the rocks and all perished. The kindly merchants turned out to be slave dealers who sold all the children on the other five ships to the Mohammedans. "But," added the survivor, "in all these years I have not known one who was willing to lighten his lot as a slave by accepting the faith of Mohammed and denying Christ." They never saw the Holy Land, but they kept the faith.

The Church, too, tried to keep the faith. To do so in the face of the failure of the crusades was not easy. Many crusaders coming home after their defeat, weary and dispirited, wondered whether the God who made this world is really good. With such doubts already in their minds they passed on the homeward journey through Bulgaria and there met people with the ideas of the old Gnostics, who, as you recall, believed that the world is bad and the body is bad. The disheartened crusaders picked up these notions and called themselves the Cathari, which means the "pure," who should have as little as possible to do with the world and with the body. They came back to southern France and soon had a large following. They were so disgusted with crusades that they would not go to war at all and would not kill even a chicken. They objected to marriage, though only a few lived up to the teaching. Since the body is evil they would make no images of the body and thus were like the Iconoclasts, though for a different reason. The Cathari went so far as to give up crosses as well as crucifixes. The worst teaching of the Cathari was that those who had reached perfection might take their own lives, lest if they lived longer they might do something wrong and spoil their records. Only a few actually killed themselves. On the whole the Cathari were good folk. An opponent of their views admitted that they cheated none, struck none and worked with their hands. Yet some of their ideas certainly were not Christian, and they called the Catholic Church a den of thieves and said that the popes were more the followers of Constantine than of Peter.

The Pope at that moment was the great Innocent III. He tried to win the Cathari back to the faith by sending preachers among them. Saint Dominic was permitted to start a new order of preachers who are named after him the Dominicans. They dressed plainly. The Pope wished them to live among the people and teach saner views. Unhappily things got out of hand. One of the preachers was murdered. The northern French were itching for a chance to gobble up southern France, which was then a country by itself. The idea of the crusade was now turned from the Turks to the heretics, that is, "those who believe the wrong way." The northern French came down pillaging and murdering, believing that they were saving their souls at the same time that they enlarged their kingdom by butchering the unbelievers. Pope Innocent had little taste for such brutality, but his power was not equal to curbing the passions of men. The Cathari were stamped out and the land was taken by northern France.

But heresy was not completely stamped out. The heretics scattered and the local clergy often would not do a thing against them, especially in places where the Catholics and Cathari had intermarried. For that reason the popes after Innocent appointed special helpers called Inquisitors who were to inquire into cases of heresy. The guilty were turned over to the government to be punished and the punishment was burning at the stake. The reason for such frightful treatment was the belief that heresy is a terrible crime against God, who would be so angered by it that He would plague the world and would burn the heretics after their death forever in hell. Burning of heretics on earth was meant to terrify others so that they would change their minds and save their souls.

The saddest part of the story is that the Church in one case made heretics out of would-be helpers. A rich merchant of southern France named Peter Waldo gave his goods to the poor and began preaching to the people. He would have been the best sort of person to win back the Cathari to the Church, but churchmen stopped him from preaching because he

was not trained. He went to Rome and appealed to the Pope, who was no wiser than the other churchmen. Waldo was ordered to stop preaching and refused to obey. He was put out of the Church. Followers came to him and he soon founded a movement known as the Waldensian. His followers sought a refuge in the highest fertile valleys of the Alps where their children's children are to this day to be found. From time to time groups of them have moved to the United States.

Happily the Church used better methods for keeping the faith. One was teaching the truth. The Church was the mother of schools and universities. We have mentioned before that the monks were teachers. They continued to train boys and young men. The instruction had to do not only with letters but also with life. Here is part of an exercise in the Latin tongue for English boys.

Boys. Master, we children ask you to teach us to speak correctly.

Master. Will you be flogged while learning?

Boys. We would rather be flogged than ignorant, but we know you are kind and will not flog us unless you have to.

Master. What work have you?

First Boy. I am going to be a monk. I sing seven times a day with the brethren. Between times I want to learn Latin.

Master. What do these companions of yours know?

First Boy. Some are ploughmen, others shepherds, some are cowherds, some too are hunters, fishermen, pedlars, merchants, shoemakers and bakers.

Master. Ploughboy, what do you do?

Ploughboy. I work very hard. At dawn I drive the oxen to the field and yoke them to the plough. Every day I have to plough an acre or more. [Then each boy is asked what he does and they begin to quarrel as to whose work is best.]

Master. Let us end this dispute. Let each help the other. Let each do his work as well as he can whether priest or monk, layman or soldier. Attend to that and be what you are. Keep the commandments of God and behave properly. Walk quietly when you hear the Church bells. In Church bow to the holy altars. Stand quietly and sing in unison and ask pardon for your sins.

The Church taught not only little boys but also older scholars. Under the leading of the Church arose the universities for the study of theology which teaches about God; philosophy which tries to understand the universe; law and medicine. The teachers in the universities were called masters and doctors. They hammered out the truth by arguing with each other.

The Church tried to keep alive the spirit of the gospels, the spirit of peace, joy and reverence. The monasteries helped. Since the days of Saint Benedict the monasteries had become very numerous. Here those who despised the turmoil of a quarrelling world might find quiet and simple living. The rule for the nuns expresses their ideal in this prayer: "Almighty God, Father, Son and Spirit, who art power, wisdom and love, inspire in me these same three things, power to serve Thee, wisdom to please Thee, and love to do it; power that I may do, wisdom that I may know what to do, love that I may be moved to do all that is pleasing to Thee."

The monasteries were popular and grew quite large. Many

people who did not join the monks yet wished to live near them with the result that a whole village grew up about a monastery. Here is a picture of a monastery in France. The village about it has been left out of the picture because the page is too small to show it all. Beginning at the left of the picture the open space inside the wall is the cemetery. The building whose roof rises out of the wall in the foreground near the cemetery is the school.

Then we come to the first gate near the church. In front of the gate is a sanctuary to which those being chased by their enemies could run and be safe. To the right of the church and toward the back of the picture are the kitchen and the dining room for the monks and another for guests. In the center toward the back is an open court with a fountain and a tree. The building just back of the tree is the brewery. From the court a passage leads under a building and past the prison for the bad monks to the middle front gate over which is built the house of the almsgiver who took care of the poor. In the right section is a wood where rabbits were raised. The building over the right front gate is the storehouse for the grain from the outlying lands. The wall seems to end behind the church because actually the wall comes there to a river and stops.

In the days of the great Pope Innocent a new kind of monasticism arose, of monks who did not call themselves monks because they did not live away from the world. They called themselves Friars or Brothers, and although they did have meetings together yet they spent most of their time with the people. The leader of the new movement was Saint Francis. He was born in the little Italian town of Assisi. His father was a rich merchant. Francis did not want to be rich. The trouble with the world, he believed, was that men were fighting over riches. And the trouble with the Church was that the monasteries had grown too rich and too comfortable and were forgetting poor folk.

Saint Francis said that he was "married to Lady Poverty." He would have absolutely nothing beyond the needs of every day. He would accept no gifts of money, only of clothes to be worn and food to be eaten. He would work, but for no wages beyond what he could eat and wear. He would beg, but not for the best, only for the worst, what others would not wear and would not eat; nor would he beg for the morrow, but only for the day. Not even the health of the body would he count as something belonging to himself, but he would go to the lepers to give them comfort even though he might catch their disease. He would go to men wherever they were, in the fields or in the cities. This was a time when cities were growing up. The followers of Saint Francis were to become great preachers, holding before the people the pattern of their Lord.

Though Francis had given up owning things he felt rich in the fair world which God has given to all, and he called on all things living to give thanks. Here are two drawings of the saint preach-

ing to the birds. One artist has shown the birds in flight. Another wished to give Francis a tough task and brought in birds of prey like the hawk and the eagle. The marks on Saint Francis' hands and feet are called stigmata. They were reddish spots which came because he thought so much about the wounds of Christ. In his sermon to the birds Saint Francis said: "Little sisters, you should praise God that He saved you in the ark and gave you the air in which to fly. You sow not, neither do you reap, but God gives you food and drink. He has given you tall trees for your nests, and because you cannot spin nor sow He has made you coats. Therefore, little sisters, be not ungrateful, but strive to praise God."

Francis himself praised God for all that He has made. Francis made a song. It is the first song in the Italian language. This is what it means in English:

O Lord, most mighty and most high,
Whom all men ought to glorify,
Though no man in his length of days
Is good enough to sing Thy praise,
Yet praised be Thou for all Thy hand
Hath wrought on sea and sky and land.
We bless Thee for our Brother Sun,
Who blazes glad his course to run,
For Sister Moon and every star,
Who choice and chaste and lovely are,
For air and cloud and gentle rain
By which Thou dost the earth sustain,
For Sister Water's gracious flow,
Useful, precious, chaste and low,
For Brother Fire who shines by night
In roaring joy and leaping light,
For Mother Earth and flowers and fruit,
For tree and shrub and herb and root,
For those whose love of Thee
Hath brought them to infirmity.
If they meekly bear their woe
Thou wilt on them a crown bestow.

Men were so drawn to Francis that they wished to live with him and to be like him. Pope Innocent gave them permission to form a new order called the Franciscan. Sister Clara founded a branch for women, known as the Poor Clares.

Many quaint tales are told of the saint's first followers. None outdo those of Brother Juniper. He was hopeless, for he would give away anything he had even to his clothes and come back blithely to the brothers for another outfit. Once a poor woman came to the friary (that is the dwelling of the friars) to ask help for her husband who was in jail for debt. She found Juniper alone. He looked to see whether there was anything to give her and spotted nothing but the silver bells on the altar cloth. "Now," thought he, "we can get along without these," and he cut them off and gave them to her. When the brothers came home and saw the damage they complained to the Father in charge. "What would you expect?" said he. "I am surprised that he left even the altar cloth. But I'll scold him. Send him in." Juniper came and the Father lectured till he was hoarse and then went to bed.

Juniper slipped down to the kitchen to make something for the Father's sore throat, but by the time it was ready the Father was asleep and had to be aroused.

"What's this, waking me up?"

"You were so hoarse from scolding me that I made this for you, Father. Now eat it. It will do you good."

"Get out and leave me alone."

"Well, Father, if you won't eat it, perhaps you will hold the candle while I eat it."

That was too much. The Father got up and they both ate.

The prayer of Saint Francis was, "O Lord, do Thou so wean my mind from all that is under heaven by the fiery and sweet strength of Thy love that I may be ready to die for the love of Thy love as Thou didst deign to die for the love of my love."

FAITH AND TEACHING

ROFOUND faith alone made possible accomplishments like those of the Church in the Middle Ages. Men believed. They believed what the early Church had believed, the Apostles' Creed and the Nicene Creed. In the course of time beliefs were worked out in greater detail with an especial fondness for the number seven. There are seven deadly sins, seven cardinal or chief virtues, seven works of mercy and seven sacraments.

The seven deadly sins are deadly because they separate man from his true nature. These seven sins are: pride, greed, luxury, envy, gluttony, anger and despair. Other sins are not so bad, such as lying and cowardice. Pictures of five of the deadly sins will be found in the next chapter on page 127. The two not shown are envy and despair which were harder to draw.

For all his sins the Middle Ages believed man would some day have to answer. Before the day of judgment the angels would blow their trumpets and the dead would get up out of the graves

to appear before the judge. The oppressed would be there to accuse the oppressors. "We were hungry," the mediæval preacher imagined they would say to Christ, "and those lords standing over there were the cause of it. We were thirsty and naked. For half the year we had no more than bread, bran and water, and worse we died of hunger, while they were served three or four courses out of the goods they took from us. They gave us not our own when we were in need. Neither did they clothe us but rather their horses, hounds and apes. O just God, O Mighty Judge, the game was not fair. Their fullness was our famine. Their mirth was our woe. Avenge, O Lord, our blood that has been shed."

Then Christ, the righteous judge, would decide the fate of those before his judgment seat. Here are the dead getting dressed to appear before him. Three possibilities would be open, to send

men to hell, to purgatory, or to heaven. Hell is a place of endless and hopeless torment. Purgatory is a place where those not good enough for heaven nor bad enough for hell may have another chance. Heaven of course is the reward of the good. A great poem of the Middle Ages describes these places. The poem is called the *Divine Comedy*. We usually think of a comedy as funny. This poem is not funny. It is called a comedy because it ends well.

The author of the poem was Dante, an Italian of Florence. The poem is made to begin on Good Friday of the year 1300. Straying into a wild forest, Dante felt the bitterness of death upon him until he climbed to an open place upon a mountain side. Here three beasts met him, a panther, a lion, and a she-wolf, which stand for uncleanness, pride, and greed. A figure appeared to guide him, the pagan poet Virgil, who lived on earth about the time of Christ. Virgil drove off the beasts and together he and Dante approached the gates of hell on which was written, "All hope give up, you who enter." In hell they found the angry, tearing each other forever and ever, and the sulky, sunk in a filthy marsh. One could tell that they were there only by the bubbles coming to the top. On Easter morning  the poet and his guide reached the gate of purgatory. Here too they found pain, but pain of a different sort, a pain that cleanses and does not last forever. At the gate of heaven Virgil had to leave because as a pagan he could not enter the abode of the blessed. A new guide now appeared, Beatrice, the Christian, who disclosed splendors before which the poet stood in rapture: the circles of the stars, the glories of the Queen of Heaven, the light supreme and pure of the Eternal King whose will is the peace of those who dwell in Paradise.

How should sinful man come to this blessed place? Devils were supposed to lie in wait to lead him into sin and to drag him over cliffs into endless torment unless the angels should rescue him as in the picture at the head of this chapter. Yet something man could do himself. If there are seven deadly sins there are also seven cardinal virtues. They are not the exact opposites of the seven sins, for the virtues were made up by taking the four virtues of the pagans: wisdom, courage, self-control, and justice, and adding to them the three Christian virtues, faith, hope, and love. Love in turn performs the seven works of mercy, which are to feed the hungry, give drink to the thirsty, clothe the naked, visit the sick, house the homeless, ransom captives, and bury the dead.

If man is to do all this he needs help and the Church provides help in the seven sacraments, through which man may have forgiveness of past sins and strength to do better. Pictures of the seven sacraments are shown on the page opposite. The first is baptism, which is given to babies. Notice the nurse putting her hand in the water to make sure that it is not too cold. Baptism is given only once. Next comes confirmation, which is like joining the Church. Notice the bishop making with his thumb the sign of the cross on the boy's forehead. Confirmation also is given only once. Penance includes confessing one's sins to the priest and trying to make them right afterwards. Sometimes this can be done directly. Stolen money, if not spent, can be given back, but many sins such as pride, greed, and envy cannot be made up. Then some-

thing else may be done, such as the seven works of mercy or going on a pilgrimage to some holy place. Penance of course can be repeated frequently. Ordination is a sacrament for the clergy and marriage for some of the laity. Ordination is possible only once. Marriage can be repeated if one partner dies. Extreme unction is an anointing given to the dying.

The sacrament most frequently held in the Catholic Church is the Mass. Most priests say it every day and Catholics try to go once a week. The Mass is the Lord's Supper. It is called Mass from the words in Latin, *Ite, missa est*, meaning, "Go, you are dis-*missed*." These words in the early Church were spoken not at the end, but just before the most sacred part of the Mass for which the beginners were not allowed to stay. The Mass has gone far beyond the Lord's Supper. The priest wears a special robe called a chasuble, and is assisted by several helpers at high Mass and one at low Mass. High Mass is so called because the words are sung by a choir in a high voice, that is, a loud voice, whereas at low Mass the words are simply said by the priest in a low voice. The people receive only the bread, never the wine. The Church in the Middle Ages took the wine away from the people lest some of the precious blood of the Christ should be spilt, for the Church believes that when the priest says the words, *Hoc est corpus meum*, which means, "This is my body," the bread is changed not outwardly but inwardly into the real body of Christ. The Mass is a true feeding on him. The Mass is also a repeating of his suffering for us. Our sins are ever crucifying him afresh, and his pain is ever renewed. The Mass is said in Latin that it may be the same throughout the world. The people in every land are taught what it means.

Yet even the sacraments of the Church do not succeed in making men perfect. They are still in need of the forgiveness of God. The Middle Ages thought of Him often as an angry God, who would not forgive unless He were persuaded. His Son who suffered on the cross would plead with Him. Yet sometimes the Son too was imagined as an angry judge unwilling to forgive. Then his mother would plead with him. The Virgin Mary was the friend of souls, and all alike, lord and lady, serf and maid, took refuge under the broad folds of the protecting Mary.

The faith of the Church in the Middle Ages was brought to the people in various ways as by plays, preaching, music and cathedrals.

Plays were written in the language of the people and gave in dramatic form the stories of the Bible, often with amusing additions by the playwright. In the play on the flood Noah's sons and

his wife and his sons' wives report as follows about the animals
which have been brought into the ark:

Shem. Sir, here are lions Libyan
  Horses, mares, ox, and swine,
  Goats, calves, sheep, and kine,
  Here thou may see.

Ham. Camels, asses, men may find,
  Buck, doe, hart, and hind;
  Beasts of every sort and kind,
  Here I think there be.

Japhet. Here are cats and dogs as well.
  Otter, fox, fullmart you smell.
  Hares by their hopping you can tell.
  And cows for to eat.

Noah's Wife. And here are bears and wolves, a set.
  Apes and owls and marmoset,
  Weasels, squirrels, and ferret:
  Here they eat their meat.

Shem's Wife. Yet more beasts are in this house!
  Here are cats, all most jocose,
  Here's a rat, and here a mouse,
  All standing high together.

  And here are fowls, all in their turn
  Hearns and cranes, and loud bittern,
  Swans and peacocks—in the stern,
  To ride the coming weather.

Japhet's Wife. Here are cocks, and kites, and crows,
  Rooks and ravens . . . many rows.
  Cuckoos, curlews, . . . whoso knows
  Each one in his kind.

And here are doves, and ducks, and drakes,
And redshanks running through your lakes,
Every fowl that sleeps and wakes,
In this ship man may find.

The animals proved much easier to bring aboard than Noah's wife herself who was unwilling to enter the ship without her friends. Her sons just in time picked her up bodily and shoved her up the gangplank.

Another way in which the Church reached the people was by preaching. The congregations gathered in the churches and sometimes in such numbers that only the out-of-doors would hold them. The preachers upbraided their flocks for their sins, held before them the seven virtues and the seven works of mercy, explained the faith and the seven sacraments and urged the people to walk in the path of life.

One of the greatest of mediæval preachers was Savonarola, a Dominican of Florence. He scathed the sins of the people and even of the churchmen  who spent their time and their wealth on hawks and hounds, tapestries and elegant lodgings, to the neglect of their flocks. When the French army was invading Italy and was about to approach the walls of Florence, the terrified people from the earliest morning thronged the great cathedral. The preacher took as his text the words from the story of the flood, "Behold I bring the water upon the earth." The people were stunned by the awful doom which he foretold for the city and went out speechless from the church. The great artist Michelangelo, who was there, never forgot the fright of that sermon and something of the feeling of it went into his painting of *The Last Judgment* years afterwards.

More comforting was the music of the Church. Bells summoned the people to worship, chiming bells. During the Mass or when carols were sung the organ pealed through nave and choir. Sometimes in songs of Christmas cheer the player let the merry  organ blow and sometimes in notes mournful and sweet the choir chanted the Virgin Mother's grief. One of the greatest hymns of the Middle Ages is called the *Stabat Mater*, written by Jacopone da Tode, a disciple of Saint Francis.

At the cross her station keeping
Stood the mournful mother weeping,
Where he hung, the dying Lord;
For her soul of joy bereavèd,
Bowed with anguish, deeply grievèd,
Felt the sharp and piercing sword.

Who, on Christ's dear mother gazing,
Pierced by anguish so amazing,
Born of woman, would not weep?
Who, on Christ's dear mother thinking,
Such a cup of sorrow drinking,
Would not share her sorrows deep?

Jesus, may her deep devotion
Stir in me the same emotion,

Fount of love, Redeemer kind:
That my heart fresh ardor gaining,
And a purer love attaining,
May with thee acceptance find.

The great center of the religious life of the people was the
Church. The Middle Ages developed the plan of the early Christian basilika. The little wings on the sides near the apse were
extended so that the ground plan came to have the form of a cross.
The early basilika had been roofed with wood. The problem was
now to make a roof of stone. The Romans had used what is called
a barrel vault. It is heavy and takes massive walls to hold it up
and has to be made all in one piece with the aid of a long scaffold-
ing. Romanesque architecture in the early
Middle Ages found a better way to build by
the use of ribbed vaulting. On four pillars
rose four ribs bending over and in to meet
each other in a knob above the center of
the square formed by the pillars. Four other
ribs rose from the same columns and by pairs
at each end, arched in to meet each other at
a point. This framework was then roofed
over. The advantage was that a section like
this could be built at one time and since the
whole push was on the pillars they alone
needed support. The Romanesque churches
made the pillars double-thick. Gothic
architecture grew out of the Romanesque
by making the vault pointed and by setting
supports for the pillars a little distance away
with arms called flying buttresses reaching

across. The roof now could be lifted to a great height. Stones seemed no longer to have weight. Ribs soared like the topmost needles of evergreens in northern forests, and the roof outside was crowded with pinnacles and spires reaching for the stars.

Windows in the Gothic cathedrals could be plentiful and large because the outside buttresses did away with the need for thick walls. The glass was set between shafts of slender stone branching at the top into leafy tracery. In the larger spaces below were set windows in colored glass done in designs to tell the story of the faith. At first each different color had to have a separate bit of glass. The pieces were leaded together. The pattern of a small window in the cathedral of Notre Dame at Paris is shown in the picture of Luxury on page 127. Notice the lead connecting her right hand with her face and her left hand with the arm of the chair. When a window was large and in many pieces the lead was not strong enough to prevent wobbling before the wind and iron bars had to be set across without regard to the pattern.

Later artists found a paint which when heated would melt right into the glass and become a part of it. Then a whole head could be painted on a single piece. Brilliant colors were used, crimson, blue and purple, often not the original tints of the object. A window at Sens, for example, of the Prodigal Son tending swine has one pig green, one blue and one red. The total effect was breath-taking as the evening sun went down behind the rose window casting soft, warm enchanting rays upon the cold gray stone.

Stories were told in the windows of the creation of the world, the flood, the sacrifice of Isaac, the crossing of the Red Sea, of Jephthah, Samson and of Jonah, then of Christ, in the manger, walking on the water, suffering on the cross, ascending to the right hand of his Father. Here was the Virgin Mother weeping over her son or exalted to heaven to be crowned by God. Here were the lives of the saints, Christopher carrying the Christ-child, Anthony fighting the devils, Augustine in his study, Jerome with his lion. All that a man really needed to know for his journey from earth to heaven was told in storied panes.

In the portals of the doorways and on ledges set into the pillars statues were placed, carved not according to the natural size and shape of the human body but taller and sometimes misshapen to give an impression of movement as of figures springing heavenward. This statue of Peter has lengthened the movable parts, the arms, the legs, and the neck, in comparison with the trunk and the head, to make the figure appear as if it were stepping right out of the stone. The statues were often painted and in this picture the artist is shown putting the paint from a bowl onto a statue of the Virgin Mary. Usually the images were of serious subjects like the characters of the Bible or the saints, but sometimes grotesque forms were used of devils or of animals. These are called gargoyles. They were especially used for water-spouts, with hideous leers spitting cloudbursts into the streets below.

After the Gothic came the Renaissance cathedral. We shall see in the next chapter what Renaissance meant. The Renaissance cathedral was something like the Byzantine in that it had a dome, but the dome itself was lifted up almost like the vaulting of the Gothic. There was this difference from the Gothic, however, that the dome had no open spaces between the ribs and in consequence the windows had to be set in below the rim of the dome. The light thus came from the bottom rather than from the top of the building. The under side of the dome, being unbroken, could be painted. Some of the great religious paintings of the Renaissance are on ceilings.

The cathedral was built by the community. To haul the materials kings and queens and men and women of high estate harnessed themselves to wagons. The heavier stones required a thousand men hitched to the same load. In silence they pulled and in unity, for if any refused to forgive another the hard-hearted one was cast out of the traces. The children had wagons of their own to pull, and chose their own kings to lead them, and, though so young, in nimbleness and speed they outdid their elders.

The cathedral was thus a spiritual home, the more so because every one helped to make it. The people pulled. The merchants gave their money. The guilds, or companies of workmen such as bakers, brewers, smiths or carpenters, presented this window or

that. The architects, artists and craftsmen vied with one another to please the Virgin in adorning her house. Viewed from a distance the cathedral with its spires and towers and flying buttresses appeared as a great ship in which man might sail to heaven. At the portal one met Christ upon the cross, the one sure Pilot. About him were ranged statues of the patriarchs and prophets of the Old Testament and the apostles and evangelists of the New, together with the martyrs, saints, monks and missionaries of the Church. Within the cathedral the soaring lines carried the eye up and up from earth to the abode of God. From that region pure and fair fell light not cold and pitiless but crimson warm upon the slabs of stone beneath which slept the dead. The Church bound together all believing souls. And here all the living came for holy festivals, the old and young, the rich and poor, the noble and the peasant, to hear the word, to watch the solemn mysteries of the faith and to chant in stately litanies the outreachings of the soul to God.

CHAPTER THIRTEEN

DEADLY SINS INVADE
THE CHURCH

FTER the great days of Innocent III and Saint Francis the Mediæval Church ran down hill. Cathedrals once built keep their imperishable charm because stone can stand the wear of wind and weather, but men may lose their quality, and the Church on earth is made up of men. The seven deadly sins invaded the Church and did more damage than the barbarians who invaded the Roman Empire. Yet just as the barbarians did not kill all the Romans, so the sins did not destroy all the virtues. In the darkest hours the candles of the faith at least flickered. We shall look at some of the ways in which the Church declined and at attempts of various kinds and in various places to restore her quality and power.

Five in particular of the seven deadly sins invaded the Church. Pictures of these five are shown on page 127. Greed is carrying off a bag of plunder. Gluttony's horse is gobbling a savory morsel. Luxury is a woman adorning herself (men did it too). Anger is about to whack a meek damsel over the head. Pride has been spilled by his horse.

The greed of the Church led to more conflicts with the State, which was greedy too, and in the struggle the Church became greedier. Bishops and abbots were rich and kings were envious. In particular the kings of England and France were building up strong countries and needed much money and were ready to take it from any who had it. The King of England helped himself to the goods of the Church and the King of France refused to let any money go from his kingdom to Rome. Pope Boniface VIII promised to excommunicate any king who took the Church's goods and any churchman who gave them, but the King of France replied by capturing the Pope and removing the Papacy to a town under French control. The name of the town was Avignon. Here the popes stayed for a little over seventy years (1305–1377). This period of absence from Rome is called the Babylonian captivity of the Papacy in memory of the captivity of the Jews for seventy years in Babylon.

Exile only increased the greed of the Church because money was harder to get. Little could be obtained from the lands of the Church in Italy which, in the absence of the popes, were overrun by neighboring rulers. The Pope at Avignon—John XXII was his name—made use of every means old and new to raise money. Fees were charged not only for baptisms, weddings and funerals, but even for such odd services as granting permission to divide a dead man and bury him in two graves. Every bishop anywhere in Europe on receiving his post was required to let the Pope take the first year's salary. If then a bishopric became vacant the Pope would move another bishop to fill the place and thus make another vacancy which would be filled by moving another bishop and making another vacancy and so on, the Pope receiving the first year's salary from them all.

Another way of getting money was from the sale of indulgences which were grants from the Pope reducing the amount of time which certain dead persons would have to spend in purgatory. The idea was that the Pope possessed a treasury of the merits of the saints, who had been better than they needed to be to get themselves out of purgatory and whose extra credits could be handed over to some one else by the Pope in return for payment by living relatives.

The deadly sin of anger entered when the Franciscans, wedded to Lady Poverty, clamored against such a pope as John XXII and called him heretic. He flared up and turned some of them over to the Inquisition to be burned. And when, too, the Italian princes took away the lands of the Church in Italy, the Pope gathered an army to fight them and spent sixty-seven per cent of his money on war.

The sins of luxury and pride came in after the Papacy returned to Rome. Then churchmen became very elegant and spent some money, to be sure, on beautiful churches and pictures and books, but more on cards and banquets, costly robes and gorgeous processions. The popes became so mighty that they had to be carried in magnificent chairs on the shoulders of warriors.

Even the monasteries, which started as a protest against the laxity of the clergy, in turn became easy-going. Saint Benedict had said that the keeper of the cellar should not be overly fond of eating, but the figure at the head of this chapter is evidently not free from the sin of gluttony.

The common folk fell from the faith of high religion to mere magic. The Lord's Supper was used like a charm. According to one story a woman kept a piece of the bread in her mouth, took it home and put it in the beehive in the hope of more honey.

Whereupon the bees built around it an entire cathedral in honeycomb. The Virgin Mary came to be regarded as a wonder worker to pull people out of scrapes. The story is told that a certain sculptor carved the likeness of a devil who lived in the church as a pediment for a statue of the Virgin. The devil was angry at being made so ugly and smashed the sculptor's ladder. He would have been killed by the fall had not the stone Virgin reached out and caught his arm. Another story of Mary's help is told in the four scenes on the next page as follows: (1) the man prays to the Virgin; (2) the crowd teases the bull; (3) the bull charges the man; (4) the Virgin stops the bull.

The deadly sins and magic in religion sapped the life of the Church. Her power grew less. Many attempts were made to amend all over Europe. In England John Wyclif tried to improve things. His idea was to get the regular priests to teach the people out of the Bible. To do so they must have the Bible in English. Wyclif persuaded several scholars to make a translation. The worst trouble was that when it was done they had no printing press to make many copies. Here is a sample of how Wyclif himself translated in his sermons. The form and spelling have been somewhat changed.

A man had two sons; and the younger of them said unto his father, Father, give me a portion of the substance that falls to me. And the father departed him his goods. And soon after, this young son gathered all that fell to him, and went forth in pilgrimage into a far country; and there he wasted his goods. And after that he had ended all his goods, there fell a great hunger in that land, and he began to be needy. And he went out, and cleaved to one of the citizens of that country, and this citizen sent him into his town, to keep swine. And this son coveted to fill his belly with peas husks that the hogs ate, and no man gave him.

Wyclif became so critical of the Church that his movement

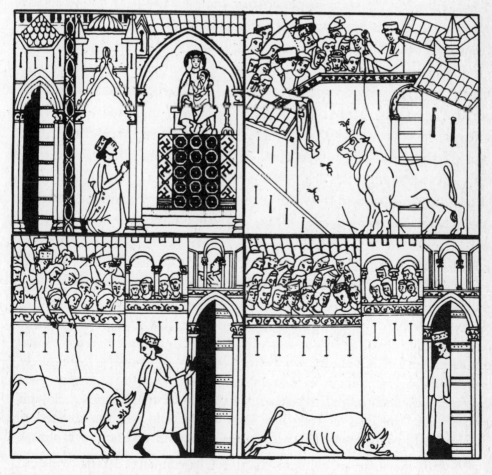

was put down in England but gained a hold in Bohemia, for the English King at that time happened to be married to a Bohemian princess. In that country John Hus preached like Savonarola against the churchmen who rode on horses with tassels streaming and kept off the people with silver clubs. For sayings like these Hus was accused of heresy and brought to trial at a council of the Church at Constance. He claimed that he had never taught what he was accused of teaching. He must take it back anyway, he was told. But how could he take back what he had never taught? He refused and was condemned to be burned. Here he is shown being led to the stake.

All Bohemia as a result flamed in revolt and actual war. Here are some of the Bohemians, fighting behind a large shield on which are carved a goblet and a goose. The goblet is the chalice or cup of the Lord's Supper, because the Bohemians insisted on giving the wine to the laity instead of the bread only. The goose stands for Hus, because Hus (pronounced Hoose) means goose.

In Spain the movement of reform was led by Cardinal Ximenes who accepted high office only when others almost dragged him from a quiet Franciscan retreat. First Queen Isabella desired him for a confessor. He consented only on condition that, when not needed to hear her confessions, he might return to the friars, but she confessed so often that the brothers soon saw him seldom. The Queen discovered that he was a wise adviser not only about the soul but also about the State. Offices were then forced upon him until he became the Chancellor of the State and a cardinal of the Church. Yet he still went barefoot and in the meanest Franciscan cowl. When on high occa-  sions the Pope ordered him to wear his gorgeous robes and cardinal's hat streaming with tassels, Ximenes obeyed, but kept next to his skin a coarse shirt of hair.

The barefoot cardinal started out to reform the friars of Spain. They must live the rule or leave the country. Queen Isabella; the General of the Franciscans at Rome and the Pope thought him too severe, but he overpowered them all with the conviction that his way was the undoubted will of heaven.

Like Wyclif he desired to spread the Bible and could do so the better because by his time printing had been discovered. Ximenes was the first to print the whole Bible in the original languages, the Old Testament in Hebrew and the New Testament in Greek. The complete work was brought out in the year 1522 and is called the Complutensian Polyglot; Complutensian because printed in the little town of Complutum and Polyglot because in more than one language. There are several copies of these books now in America.

The printing press was used for many other religious books besides the Bible. A group of men called Humanists undertook to print the works of the early leaders of the Church all of whose writings up to this time had, of course, been only in manuscripts.

Here is one of the Humanists in his study. Notice the flowers on his desk. Now for the first time Saint Augustine was printed, and Saint Jerome and Saint Ambrose and many more. The idea was abroad that the declining Church and the declining world needed to be reborn by going back to the great days of old Greece and Rome and of the early Church. This rebirth is called the Renaissance.

One of the greatest of the Humanists of the Renaissance was Erasmus of Rotterdam in Holland. He did not care where he was born, for he wanted to belong to all the world. He did more than any other to print the works of the Church Fathers and he has the honor of having first printed the New Testament in Greek by itself. This was in 1516, six years before Ximenes brought out the entire Bible in the original tongues.

Erasmus also retold the Bible stories in simple language. Here is an example of a part of the parable of the Prodigal Son from an early English translation of his work:

The young man ariseth. Back goeth he, therefore, home again, all the way he had come, weeping and sighing all the way. Whereas he had before departed from his father as pert and fierce and as rash and wilful as could be. Thou hast thou a plain pattern and example declared unto thee of a man returning from extreme naughtiness: now behold a pattern of the gracious mercifulness of God. The young man was not full come to his father's house when the father espied him coming afar off. He that did more tenderly love of the two did first espy the other. He saw his son coming, wondrous ugly and piteous to behold. He saw him ragged, hungry-starven, filthy, lamenting, sighing and weeping. This very sight being so piteous began by and by to move the father's heart. He runneth forth to meet the young man, as the same was coming towards him, and caught his son about the neck and kissed him.

Erasmus was a preacher who poked gentle fun at the magical religion of the people and scorched the deadly sins of churchmen. The folly of trusting to the saints to get us out of scrapes is shown in the story which he told of a shipwreck. The waves were heaving the vessel almost up to the moon and dropping it again as if it were sinking to hell. Many of the passengers prayed to the saints and to the Virgin Mary for help. A fat Frenchman called in a loud voice to the statue in Paris of Saint Christopher, the patron saint of travellers, promising, if saved, to give the saint a candle as big as himself. A by-stander nudged the Frenchman and suggested he should not promise too much. "Oh," said he in a low tone, lest Saint Christopher should hear, "fool, do you think I mean what I say? If I once get to shore, I will not give him as much as a tallow candle." The story teller was asked whether he would not pray to the saints. "No," said he, "for Saint Peter, who would perhaps hear the soonest, is at the gate of heaven, and while he was going to tell God, I might go to the bottom. I am going to speak to God straight." When the ship broke up, one man took hold of a wooden, worm-eaten image of the Virgin, which soaked up with water and took him to the bottom. A woman with a little child was strapped to a stout plank. She got to shore. So did the story teller, of course, who preferred a bag of cork to a golden candlestick.

Against the greed and warlike anger of churchmen Erasmus grew hot. War, especially when led by popes for the sake of the goods of the Church, seemed to him clean contrary to the spirit of Christ. The monk in armor was for him the very worst denial of the way of Jesus. "How is it," said he, "that when Christ said, 'My peace I leave with you,' the followers of Christ go out to battle with the cross on their banners and even cannons are stamped with the names of the Apostles, Peter and Paul?"

The lights were dim but in many a corner a candle was burning. Along the valley of the Rhine river in Germany was a group of quiet folk who called themselves the Friends of God. They did not start a Church of their own, nor a monastery, but they kept in touch with one another and tried to revive the love of their

Lord. Another similar group in Holland called themselves "The Brethren of the Common Life." They usually lived together and shared their goods, spending most of their time in teaching. Some spread their ideal by teaching one here one there in schools and universities. From this group came a book which has been almost as much translated and read as the Bible. It is called "The Imitation of Christ." We are not perfectly sure which brother wrote it, but the author is commonly supposed to have been Thomas à Kempis.

The theme of the book is love.

There is nothing sweeter than love, nothing stronger, nothing higher, nothing broader, nothing more profound, nothing fuller, nothing better in heaven nor in earth; for love is born of God. Love gives all things for all things and has all things in all things. Love feels no burden and takes account of no labor. It never complains of the impossible but regards itself as mighty to do all things. Love wakes, and, sleeping, is not asleep. Love is wearied, but not weary, and, when affrighted, is not troubled. Love is sweet, pure, holy, merry, strong, patient, true, prudent, long-abiding, and never seeking itself. If any man seeks himself, he falls from love. Love is discreet, meek, and right, not soft, nor light, nor given to vain things; sober, chaste, steady, and respectful. He who is not ready to suffer all things and to stand at the will of his beloved is not worthy to be called a lover.

Some of the brightest candles were kept burning by ordinary people like this girl who went about her daily tasks such as spinning and who in her room prayed that God would revive again the love and goodness of His Church.

LUTHER REVOLTS

ERHAPS if all these earnest persons in different lands had worked along quietly the Church might have been reformed without being split. No one can tell what might have happened. The Church was split because of a man who thought that the trouble with the Church lay deeper than other people seemed to see. Erasmus poked fun at the magic of the saints. Ximenes drove easy-going friars out of Spain. The Brethren of the Common Life tried by teaching to build up a better quality of Christian youth. A German monk named Martin Luther believed that none of the others had touched bottom. What is religion all about? he asked. Religion has to do with how man stands before God. But God is great and man is little. God is strong and man is weak. God is good and man is sinful. How then can little man ever stand before God and claim anything from Him? God is the Father Almighty, the Creator of the heavens and the earth, who has given man the gift of life that he might use and enjoy the good earth.

And man has wrecked it. Swollen with pride and greed he has crushed his fellows. If man is sorry how can he ever make things right? If from now on he does all that he can, that will be no more than he ought to have done anyway. There is thus no chance ever to do anything extra to make up for the wrong. Man cannot help himself. Where then is he? His only hope is in God who has shown His love in Christ and who through Christ will forgive man no matter how bad he may be if only he will trust in God. This is the meaning of Luther's watchword that we are saved by faith and not by works. We are able to get right with God not by what we do but by our trust in Him.

Luther was a monk and tried his best to be a good one. He was also a teacher at a university and at the same time a preacher in the little town of Wittenberg in a part of Germany called Saxony. He found that the members of his congregation were buying indulgences. The matter came about in this way. Albert of Brandenberg was not old enough to be a bishop at all, but he was already bishop in two places at once and got money from both. Now he wanted a third post. The Pope was willing provided Albert would pay twelve thousand ducats for the twelve Apostles. Albert said he was paying only for the seven deadly sins and would give seven thousand. The Pope came down to ten thousand, but Albert did not have so much and had to borrow it from the bankers. To enable him to pay it back the Pope permitted an indulgence sale in his lands, half to go to Albert and half to the Papacy to build the church of Saint Peter in Rome.

Luther probably did not know all this, but he knew enough and was shocked with the very idea of indulgences. You recall that the indulgence was supposed to release certain dead persons from so many years of purgatory by transferring to them the extra credits of the saints. Luther declared that no one has any extra

credits, not even the saints. In order to start a discussion Luther followed the custom of writing out his ideas and nailing the parchment to the door of the church at Wittenberg. This he did in the year 1517 and by so doing he started the Protestant Reformation. The statement which he posted is called the Ninety-Five Theses because it had many paragraphs. In it Luther said that there is no such thing as a treasury of stored-up credits; that those who are really sorry for having done wrong will be ready to suffer in purgatory; and that if the Pope knew how poor the Germans were he would rather that the church of Saint Peter should lie in ashes than that it should be built out of the blood of his sheep.

Luther did not expect anything very exciting to happen. He hoped that the university leaders and churchmen would debate the idea of indulgences. But soon all Germany was discussing the question. The Ninety-Five Theses were turned into German and given to the printing press. Few Germans understood all that Luther was trying to say, but they did understand that the money from the sale of indulgences went out of Germany

to Rome. They could grasp a cartoon which contrasted Christ driving out the money changers and the Pope receiving the money.

The Pope soon saw that the matter was serious. Nevertheless, he was slow in doing anything about it because he did not wish to anger the Germans and their princes. Perhaps things might have quieted down if Luther had not been led in a debate to attack the power of the Pope himself. In the debate Luther was asked whether his views were not the same as those of John Hus. "Heavens, no!" exclaimed Luther, but on thinking the matter over decided they were. "Very well, then," came the retort, "you agree with a heretic condemned by a pope. Was the Pope wrong in condemning Hus?" Luther answered that the Pope was wrong and that popes may be wrong and only the Bible is always right.

On the preceding page Luther is shown holding up the Bible against the Pope, who has a broken key and sits in a tottering chair.

But if the Bible alone is to be followed rather than the Pope as the successor of Saint Peter, then the Church should try to pattern herself after the Bible and should give up what the Bible does not teach. The attempt to follow the Bible led Luther to give up many practices of the Catholic Church.

First came an attack on the Mass. The Bible teaches a Lord's Supper, but no Mass. Christ said, "This is my body." This means that the bread is already his body, not that the bread is changed into his body when the priest says certain words. Christ said, "Drink ye all of it," which means that every one should take the wine and not the priest only. At this point Luther was following Hus. Christ did not say that his suffering for mankind is repeated every time in the Lord's Supper. And Christ did not say that the service could be said only in Latin. It might as well be in German.

Christ did not found seven sacraments, according to Luther, but only two, baptism and the Lord's Supper. The other five are not sacraments. But that does not mean that they are all to be given up. Some may be given up, such as extreme unction for the dying. But marriage is not to be given up, even if it is not to be a sacrament. The reason it is not a sacrament is that marriage holds among all peoples, whereas sacraments belong only to Christians.

Marriage should be kept; monasteries should be given up, said Luther. Monks, nuns and clergymen should be free to marry if they wish. In the old days when all the world was disordered by the barbarian invasions there was some point in leaving the world. But now that Europe has become a Christian society, said he, let Christians stay in the world and do the work, whatever it be, to which God has called them, whether as shoemakers, parents, teachers, rulers and even soldiers.

How could Luther's plan for such a reform of the Church be carried out? The Pope could not be expected to do it. Some bishops perhaps might. Many would not. Luther turned to the State. Just as the Papacy in its beginnings had been helped by the State so now was the Protestant Reformation. The State, however, which gave a hand to the reform was not the Holy Roman Empire. The State itself was divided. The Holy Roman Empire was on the side of the Holy Catholic Church. The State which helped Luther was the little German state of Saxony and the princes of Saxony thereby ran the risk of being punished by the Emperor. The prince of Saxony in Luther's day was Frederick the Wise. The Emperor was Charles V. He had the same name as Charles the Great (Charlemagne) and he had an even greater empire. Charles was a sincere Catholic who would rather lose his lands than have them tainted by heresy. Frederick the Wise only partly understood what Luther meant. Frederick did sense that Luther was a deeply religious man. Frederick as a German did not want to see German money go to Rome. And as a German

prince he wanted to see his subject given a fair hearing. Here is a picture of Luther and one of the German princes kneeling before the crucifix.

By 1520 the Pope saw that the time had come to act. Luther had attacked not only indulgences, but also the sacraments and the right of the Pope himself to decide for the Church. Luther was excommunicated. He replied by throwing the decree of excommunication on a bonfire. Excommunication did no more than separate one from the sacraments of the Church. If there were any other punishment the State had to do it. The next move against Luther, then, was to have him condemned by the Holy Roman Empire, whose officers were about to gather in a meeting called a diet in the German city of Worms. This is called the Diet of Worms. To this meeting Luther should be sent for a trial. Frederick the Wise was determined that he should be fairly heard and secured a promise that he would be returned safely home, but the promise was good for only forty days.

In April, 1521, Luther stood before the princes of Germany and the Holy Roman Emperor, Charles the successor of Charlemagne, a staunch believer in the Catholic faith. Luther was shown a pile of his books on a table and asked to take back everything in them. He checked the list and said that the books were his, but as for taking back everything in them he would have to think that over. As a great favor he was given until the next day. On the morrow he spoke to the diet: "Most serene Emperor and most noble lords, if I make any mistake in your proper titles please forgive me. I have lived in a monastery, not a court. As for my books they are of three kinds. First there is what I have said of the Christian belief and life. Even the bull against me admits that some of my teaching is harmless. If then I should take it all back I should be taking back what every one accepts. Secondly there is what I have said about all the money that goes out of Germany. If I should take that back and you German princes approved, poor Germany would get worse treatment. Thirdly there is what I have said against people. I admit I have been too hot, but I am not being judged on my life but on my teaching. And now I would remind you of what happens when princes act like Pharaoh and the King of Babylon. May the reign of Prince Charles begin in the fear of God."

"Brother Martin," replied the examiner, "you haven't divided your works enough. You should have divided them into those which are bad and those which are worse. Of course there is some good in what you say. That makes it all the worse, because people will be deceived the more easily. And who are you to think you know everything and all the teachers of the Church for so many centuries have been wrong? The faith was given by Christ, taught by the Apostles, sealed by the blood of the martyrs, worked out by the doctors and councils and given to us by the Pope and the Emperor to be believed. Now do you or do you not take back your teaching? Give us an answer without horns."

Luther answered, "Since your Majesty and your Lordships ask for a plain answer I will give you one without either horns or teeth. Unless I am shown by the Bible or reason—I do not trust in popes and councils since they have often made mistakes—unless I am shown out of the Bible I neither can nor will take back anything. My conscience is a captive to the Bible and I cannot go against conscience. God help me. Amen."

Charles spoke the next day saying, "The emperors before me were true sons of the Catholic Church and I would rather lose all my lands and even my life than go against the Christian faith. A single monk here sets himself against what the Church has believed for a thousand years and more. After his stiff-necked reply of yesterday I am sorry I have toyed with him so long. He shall be allowed to go home in accord with the promise, but after that any one who finds him is to turn him over to the officers."

Luther had not waited to hear this. He had already left the night before. As he approached the Black Forest with a few companions some horsemen dashed out and seized him. His followers fled. The news spread that he had been killed. But Luther's friends by and by began to get letters with the address, "Among the birds." What had happened was that Frederick the Wise called in one of his men and said, "I want you to hide Luther. And don't tell me where he is. I don't want to be able to answer any questions." Arrangements were made that Luther should hide in the castle of the Wartburg. He gave up his cowl, let his beard grow, dressed like a knight and drank beer with the neighbors without telling them who he was except that they sometimes wondered when they saw him with a Hebrew Bible.

Forced into hiding, Luther spent his time well. Perhaps his greatest work was the translation of the Bible into the German tongue which he began at the Wartburg. He made Moses talk like a German. Instead of translating the Psalm, "Lift up your heads O ye gates," Luther gave it a form which would make sense to the men of Wittenberg, "Make wide the gates and high the doors." The greatness of Luther's translation, however, lies not just in the choice of expressions easy to be understood by the men of his time and town but much more because he had lived over again that of which the Biblical writers spoke. How else could he have rendered the seventy-third psalm like this? "What do I care for heaven if Thou art not there? On earth I care for nothing if only I have Thee. I would not be in heaven if Thou wert not there, and with Thee would I gladly be in hell. If only I have Thee I care neither for heaven nor hell, that is neither for good nor ill. My heart faints and is consumed. Body and soul languish within me. When all goes wrong I cleave to Thee. Thou art my comfort."

While Luther was in hiding some of his friends at Wittenberg started carrying out his ideas much more quickly and roughly than he thought wise and fit. Students rioted and pelted the priests with stones. Luther decided that the time had come for him to go home and quiet things down. Never in his life was he more brave. He had no permission to go home. If any one caught him he could be turned over to the State to be burned at the stake. Luther wrote to Frederick the Wise: "I am coming home. I am not asking you to protect me. If I thought you would protect me with the sword I would not come. If the Emperor comes after me do not stand in his way, though you need not hand me over to him of your own accord." The Emperor proved too busy to come for twenty-five years. He was busy fighting the Turks and the French and the Pope. The most Catholic ruler who had said he would rather lose lands and life than do anything against the Christian faith was actually fighting the head of the Christian Church over the control of Italy. The troops of Charles got out of hand and sacked Rome and captured the Pope. Though he was soon released, these events explain how Luther was free to start the Lutheran Church. More slowly than the student rioters, but none the less surely with the aid of the Saxon princes Luther stopped the Mass, and ended the monastic orders. The Church services were simplified and turned into German. The clergy and the monks and nuns began to get married. The new movement was given the name Protestant in 1529 when the reformers *protested* against an order of the diet of the Empire that their work should spread no further. The movement did spread and the unity of the Church of the Middle Ages was broken.

As once the Greek and the Latin had separated so now the northern peoples of Europe separated from the southern, for the Protestant movement was soon to have its greatest strength in Germany, Denmark, Norway, Sweden and England, whereas the Catholic Church kept its hold in Italy, Spain and France in the main. Catholicism held the lands of the old Roman Empire where God was called *Dio* and *Dieu* from the Latin *Deus*. Protestantism spread among the peoples more directly of the barbarian stock who called the Father Almighty *Gott* and *God*. The exception was Ireland, which stayed with the Catholic Church because of disagreement with England.

Like other monks Luther married. His wife was a former nun. They had six children. Luther enjoyed his home and was fond of his children. Even though Luther did once cut up Hans' pants to mend his own, the father would surely be forgiven when he wrote to his little boy a letter like this:

April 22, 1530

To my dear son, Hans Luther:

Grace and peace in Christ, my darling little son. I am very glad to hear that you are studying well and praying diligently. Go on doing so, my little son, and when I come home I will bring you a beautiful present.

I know a lovely, pretty garden, where there are many children. They wear golden coats, and pick up fine apples, pears, cherries and plums under the trees. They sing and jump and are very merry. They also have beautiful little horses with bridles of gold and saddles of silver. I asked the man who owned the garden who the children were. He answered,

"These are the children who gladly pray and study and are good." Then I said, "Dear man, I also have a son named Hans Luther. Wouldn't he like to come into the garden and eat such beautiful apples and pears and ride such fine horses and play with these children?" Then the man said, "If he prays and studies gladly, and is good, he too shall come into the garden, and Lippus and Jost with him. And when they are all here they shall have whistles and drums and lutes, and all sorts of things to make music with, and they shall dance and shoot with little crossbows." And he showed me a beautiful meadow in the garden fixed for dancing. Gold whistles were hung there, and drums and silver crossbows. But it was still early and the children had not yet eaten, so I couldn't wait for the dance, and I said to the man: "Dear sir, I will go as fast as I can and write it all to my dear son Hans, that he may study and pray well and be good and so come into this garden. But he has an Aunt Lena whom he will have to bring with him." Then the man said, "Very well, go and write it to him."

Therefore, dear little son Hans, study and pray bravely, and tell Lippus and Jost to do so too, and you shall come into the garden with each other. The dear God take care of you. Greet Aunty Lena and give her a kiss for me.

Your loving father,
Martin Luther.

Luther's little daughter Elizabeth died as a baby. Luther wrote to a friend, "My little Elizabeth, my wee daughter, is dead. It is wonderful how sorrowful she has left me. My soul is almost like a woman's, so moved am I with misery. I could never have believed that the hearts of parents are so tender toward their children. Pray the Lord for me."

Luther was a mighty warrior, often a rough and coarse fighter. His preaching was as the roaring of a lion. On the next page he is thundering in the pulpit. He was also a singer and, like Saint Ambrose in the basilika, knew that a singing congregation could defy

any foe. The little Lutheran Church still had many and dangerous
foes. Toward the end of Luther's life the Emperor had a free hand
and marched with his army to Germany to crush the Protestant
movement. Many of the ministers were driven out. Luther escaped that fate by death. Luther's prince was taken captive. A
few years after, however, the Emperor had to retreat and the
Lutheran movement revived. For such trying times Luther wrote
the stirring hymn:

A mighty fortress is our God
A bulwark never failing;
Our helper He amid the flood
Of mortal ills prevailing.
For still our ancient foe
Doth seek to work us woe;
His craft and power are great
And, armed with cruel hate,
On earth is not his equal.

Did we in our own strength confide,
Our striving would be losing;
Were not the right man on our side,
The man of God's own choosing.
Dost ask who that may be?
Christ Jesus, it is he.
Lord Sabaoth his Name,
From age to age the same,
And he must win the battle.

CHAPTER FIFTEEN

REFORMERS REFORMED

EFORM was in the air in Luther's day and the notes from his bugle awoke many who were only waiting for a signal to reform their own Churches and if need be to separate from the Catholic Church. These people, however, did not join the Lutheran Church but started Churches of their own. Often they went much farther than Luther in giving up the practices of the Catholic Church. These newer Protestant groups are called in general "reformed" Churches. They arose in Switzerland, a little country where people of French and German speech live together in peace. The religious question divided them and in this instance the Germans did not all turn Protestant, nor did the French all stay Catholic. In France itself Protestantism for long was to have a strong footing and only in a rough way can we say that Protestantism was accepted by the Germanic and Catholicism by the Latin peoples.

Three churches had their rise in Switzerland. The first began in German Switzerland at Zürich and is called simply the Reformed. The second began in the same place and called itself the Baptist Church. It was to spread into other parts of Europe, particularly Holland, and later to England and America. The third church began in French Switzerland in the town of Geneva under the leadership of John Calvin and is called the Presbyterian. Later it was to be strong in France, Holland, Scotland, England and America. In Holland it was called the Dutch Reformed Church.

In this chapter we shall look at the two Churches which began in Zürich. The leader of the Reformed Church in that town was Zwingli. Like Luther he objected to the sale of indulgences and to the unmarried state of the clergy. Zwingli like Luther married. And like Luther he believed that the Catholic Church had fallen away from the pattern of the Bible and that the Pope was misusing the keys of Saint Peter. A Swiss cartoon showed Saint Peter wrestling with the Pope to get the keys back.

Zwingli made even more of the Bible as a pattern for the Church than did Luther. The Catholic practice which had been followed by the Lutheran was to read only certain parts of the Bible in church each Sunday. Zwingli instead started his preaching in Zürich in the year 1519 by going through the Gospel of Matthew verse by verse from end to end. Nor did he use any one else's translation but had the original Greek printed by Erasmus in front of him on the pulpit and explained its meaning to the people  in his own words. The discovery of America by Columbus did not cause as much excitement in Zürich. For over a thousand years parts of the Bible had not been known by the people. Now to discover again lost parts of the Word of God was more thrilling than to find unknown parts of the earth's surface.

The Bible had been accepted by Luther as the rule for Protestants and the Church was to be brought into accord with this rule, but in carrying out the idea Zwingli went far beyond Luther, for Luther said what the Bible does not forbid we may do. Zwingli said what the Bible does not command we may not do. For that reason Zwingli gave up all images and crosses in the churches. In this respect he was like the Iconoclasts. Organs in church also were given up. The Lutherans loved to sing around the organ. The Zwinglians, if they sang at all, did so without any instrument.

The greatest difference was with regard to the Lord's Supper. Luther, although he gave up the Mass of the Catholic Church, nevertheless believed that the body of Christ is in the bread and the wine. Christ said, "This is my body." So it is his body. The words which the priest says do not make it his body. It just is his body. But Zwingli said that Christ no more meant that the bread and the wine are his body than he meant to call himself a tree when he said, "I am the true vine." The bread and the wine simply stand for his body and the Lord's Supper is a reminder of his suffering for us.

Religious changes in Zürich, as in Wittenberg, were brought about by the State, only the State was different. Switzerland was not ruled by the Holy Roman Empire and Zürich was not governed by princes like Frederick the Wise, but rather by a council of the representatives of the people. The government was democratic. A debate between the Catholic and Protestant leaders was staged before the council at Zürich. Zwingli was the Protestant speaker. The Catholic leader refused to debate. "This council," he said, "has no right to change Christianity. Can Zürich decide for France, Spain and Italy? Then, too, the universities should be heard, Paris for example."

"And Wittenberg," put in Zwingli, who claimed that Christianity was not being changed. The Protestants were simply going back to the true form of the Bible. They did not need to ask what any one else thought about it, because they had the clear word of God on the table in Hebrew, Greek and Latin.

The council decided in Zwingli's favor. The Mass was stopped. Images and organs were removed. An old Catholic custom was given up, that of going without meat during the forty days before Easter, called Lent. Christoph Froschower, the printer, went ahead and took meat, saying that he had to have enough strength to finish printing the New Testament by Easter. Here is the design which he put on the first pages of all his books. The frog stands for the first part of his name, *Frosch*, which in German means frog. Notice the skyline of Zürich in the distance across the lake.

Other cities of German Switzerland joined the Reform. In the town of Bern the people were persuaded by pageants. In one of these shows two peasants were seen standing on the sidelines as a procession passed of a man poorly clad riding on a donkey followed by a sad-looking throng of the poor, maimed and the blind.

Here is the dialogue.

First Peasant. Who is that poor fellow on the donkey? He wears a plain gray cloak and on his head he has a wreath of thorns. The poor, the lame and the blind follow him. He turns none away. For all he has a word of cheer and he rides so humbly on his beast. Tell me who he is for Jesus' sake.

Second Peasant. Why, that's just who he is, gentle, meek, kind, comforting and full of cheer. He is the Savior of the world, our Lord Jesus Christ.

The procession passes on and is followed by another of horsemen and footmen with blowing of trumpets and beating of drums.

First Peasant. Who is the mighty Emperor followed by so many soldiers? Were it not for the priests I'd say they were Turks with their elegant clothes, red, black, brown and blue. Some have red hats and some coal black. The leader has a three-layer crown of gold. He rides on a horse and is warlike and wild. Can you tell me who he is?

Second Peasant. Why yes, he is the representative on earth of the man on the donkey.

In Basel, another town of Switzerland, the common folk took things into their own hands and rioted against the images in the churches. In one day every image in the public places of the town was smashed except one. A statue of the Virgin and her babe on the town gate was overlooked. When the oversight was noticed the people had cooled down and let it stay. There to this day the Virgin smiles not only upon her child but upon those who pass below through the gate, be they Protestant, Catholic or Jew.

Certain parts of Switzerland, however, stayed strongly Catholic. Some of their lands overlapped those of Zürich. In this territory Catholics and Protestants began to treat each other with killings and burnings. The outcome was war. In the first conflict good sense won. Peace was made on the field of battle, one side bringing bread and the other milk for a huge bowl of bread and milk. But the next time the Catholics came in great numbers and surprised the Protestants. Many of the rulers and ministers of Zürich were left dead upon the field of battle, among them Zwingli himself.

Some of the Protestants at Zürich felt that this disaster was a punishment for taking up arms on behalf of the gospel religion. Did not Jesus say, "If any one strike you on the right cheek turn to him the other also?" These people were the Baptists. They had been followers of Zwingli and had met with him to find out what an exact following of the Bible would mean. Nowhere in the Bible could they find a clear word commanding that babies be baptized. The Bible says "Go ye into all the world and baptize all peoples." But it does not say, "Baptize all babies."

And why should babies be baptized? What does baptism mean and what good does it do? In the days of the Apostles baptism was an initiation into the Church. In that case, said these people, it should be given only to those who have made up their own minds that they want to be initiated into the Church and not to every baby that happens to be born in Zürich. Infant baptism is no baptism, said they, and began, therefore, to baptize each other. But because they had already been baptized as babies the name Anabaptist, meaning *Over-again-baptizer*, was fastened on them. Their own name for themselves was simply Baptist.

Soon they were driven out of the churches and had to meet in fields and forests. Later in Holland they met for worship in boats, as this old picture shows them. On shore are the churches from which they had been driven out. In the stern of the boat some

people are reading from the Bible. At the bow others are talking and pointing, probably to conceal what the rest were doing.

One may doubt whether the Anabaptists would have been so hated, feared and maltreated if they had done nothing more than refuse to baptize babies. They went further and separated Church and State. "What did Christianity in Bible times have to do with the State?" they asked. "Of course, nothing," answered the other side. "But things are different now. The State has become Christian." "Has it indeed?" said the Anabaptists. "Are all the officers really Christian? Are all the people in Zürich really Christian? Are all the Church members even Christian? They are not. The true followers of Christ are few. But they alone ought to be the Church. The State, however, does and should include everybody. But in that case the Church and the State cannot be one."

"But why do you say that the State is not Christian?" the other side asked.

"Because for one reason the State goes to war," they answered, "whereas Jesus told us to love our enemies. Also because the State calls upon us to swear while Jesus said, 'Swear not at all.'" Swearing, as they used the word, did not mean using bad words but was the same as an oath which is bolstering up a promise by giving God leave to do something dreadful if the promise is not kept. It's like, "Cross my heart and hope to die," or "Hope the worms'll eat me when I'm dead." Jesus said a plain yes or no ought to be enough.

Because of all these teachings about baptism, the separation of Church and State, war and the oath, the Anabaptists were punished under the old law of Justinian which put to death the Donatists for repeating baptism. Protestant and Catholic alike turned against the Anabaptists. In Protestant lands they were drowned. In Catholic lands they were sometimes drowned, sometimes burned. Such punishments did not crush but scattered the movement. One branch, the Hutterites, after many and long wanderings in Europe, found a home in the United States and in Canada. Another group sprang up in the Netherlands. They came to be known as Mennonites. For a time they were severely treated in Holland. Spain was ruling the country at that time and Spain was savagely Catholic.

We have the account of the trial in Holland of a young Mennonite woman named Elizabeth. Here is a part of the record.

On the 15th of January in the year 1549 Elizabeth was taken. The examiner asked her on oath if she had a husband. She answered, "I cannot take an oath. All I can say is yes and no!"

"What persons have you taught?"

"I cannot tell you. I will confess my faith."

"We will torture you."

"I hope that with God's help I shall keep my tongue and not be a traitor."

"What do you think of the Most Holy Sacrament?"

"I have never in my life read in the Bible of a Most Holy Sacrament. I have read only of the Lord's Supper."

"Why have you been baptized again?"

"I haven't been baptized again. I have simply been baptized."

"Do you think baptism saves you?"

"No. All the waters in the sea cannot save me. Christ saves me."

Then they tortured her with thumb screws till the blood gushed from her nails and she fainted. Coming to herself she would not give in. Then she was sentenced in the year 1549 on the 27th of March to be put to death by drowning.

The sufferings of the Anabaptists were not without fruit. The Dutch came to see that they were good folk and when Holland gained independence from Spain the Mennonites were permitted their own worship. They have many churches in Holland today. In the United States the Mennonites are strong in Pennsylvania and Indiana.

modio, ſed vt in candelabro

Non accenditur lucerna vt ſub

ponatur. MATTH. V.

A CHOSEN PEOPLE

NABAPTISM was matched in its zeal for a pure Church by Presbyterianism. The word Presbyterian comes from a Greek term meaning elder, and this Church was called Presbyterian because its affairs were managed not by bishops but by elders. The Lutheran Church like the Catholic had bishops, who ruled sections of the Church much as the German princes ruled sections of Germany. The Presbyterian Church placed its government in the hands of the older men, called elders, who formed councils like those which governed the Swiss cities. Each church had a board of elders and a group of churches had a council of selected elders called a Presbytery.

The Presbyterian Church is frequently called Calvinist because its founder was John Calvin. He was a Frenchman who fled from France because Protestantism was being persecuted in that country. His hope was to find a quiet spot where he could carry on his studies. Although only in his twenties he had written a book which became the primer of Protestantism. Its title is *The Institutes of the Christian Religion*. The book appeared in Latin and in French and the French in which it was written did much to help the growth of the language. John Calvin would have been glad to settle down and write further books, the more so because his health was poor. He was frail, suffering from several diseases, including frightful headaches. But just as Ximenes was almost dragged from a Franciscan monastery to be the leader of Church and State in Spain, so John Calvin was drafted to be the head of the Protestant community of Geneva. The Reformation had already been introduced in the city, but was having a rocky time. When the call came to be pilot of the ship Calvin would gladly have said no, but the duty was laid on him as a word from God and he shouldered the load. He was soon to be preaching, teaching school, and attending to endless trying matters in a troubled time. Here is a picture of him which was drawn by one of the boys in his school.

The task which Calvin undertook was a difficult one because the Reformation was in danger from without and from within. From without there was the threat of Catholic France. Protestantism had as yet only a slight hold in that country. The Protestants there were called Huguenots. Just where the name came from no one knows. They were being burned at the stake or driven out of the country. There was danger even that the whole city of Geneva might be captured by the armies of France. The city would have been quite easy to nip off because it was on the tip of a wedge of Protestant land thrust into the midst of Catholic

France. Throughout Calvin's lifetime the city was in constant fear of attack and even after his death an assault was made though it failed. Here is a sketch of Geneva from an old drawing. The high tower belongs to the cathedral where Calvin preached.

The Protestants of Geneva found great comfort in the stories of the Old Testament about the children of Israel who also were beset about with many foes, the Amorites, the Hivites, Jebusites, Philistines. The Calvinists called their children after the Old Testament characters rather than after the saints of the Catholic Church. When some parents wished to christen a son Claude they were compelled instead to call him Abraham. On coming to America Calvinists named their towns after Old Testament places such as Dan, Gilead, Hebron, New Canaan and Mount Carmel. As the Israelites were saved under Gideon or David through the power of the Lord of hosts even so would the town of Geneva be

secure under Calvin through the protecting care of the Eternal.

But the people must be faithful to Him as were the Israelites of old. For God's sake Abraham had left his country and kindred and his father's house to go into a land which God should show him. That same Abraham had been willing to sacrifice his only son at God's command. A play about Abraham and Isaac was written in French and acted at Geneva. The Bible story was enlarged to bring out the struggle of the old man called upon, as he believed, by God to take the life of the son of his love. Abraham raised his dagger to strike but let it fall exclaiming:

> And was there ever yet so piteous case?
> I die, my son, I die before thy face.
>
> .   .   .   .
>
> Alas, my son, I pray thee me forgive
> Thy death. It kills me that thou may not live.

Again Abraham lifted his knife, when this time the angel called from the thicket.

Abraham was a favorite among the Calvinists not only because he was so faithful but also because God saved his son Isaac and made him the father of a people very precious to God, a chosen people. This was first the Jewish people, then the Christian, who were children of Abraham not by blood but in the spirit. When later many Christians fell away the true line passed to the Calvinists. They were the chosen people.

They must, then, act like it and must permit none among them to offend in creed or in deed. Those who did not believe in the reformed faith must leave the city. One of the citizens did not know quite what to do. He loved Geneva, but he did not feel sure that the Catholic Church was all wrong. He was told that if he did not go to Protestant Church services he would be put out of the town in ten days. Then the order was changed so that he would be put in prison from which he would be taken every day to church. Geneva had church every day. This would be done to him unless he would say, "The Mass is bad." He replied that he was not able to judge, but since the council said the Mass is bad he would say the Mass is bad. That was not enough. He must say simply, "The Mass is bad." He said it and stayed. Others left.

Actions as well as beliefs had to measure up to the standard of the Reformed Church. In ancient Israel those who offended were put out of the camp. So should it be in the new Israel. One of the members of the Church was refused permission to come to the Lord's Supper unless he mended his ways. The town council gave him permission to commune. Here was a case in which the State was interfering with the rules of the Church. Calvin answered that this was no question for the town council to decide. Rather than give in he would leave the city. Sunday came. Calvin mounted the pulpit and said, "If any one comes to this communion table who has been put out by the Church, I will do my duty with my life." Calvin, pale, thin, worn, looked out over the congregation to see whether the offender would come forward. He did not come. Calvin had won.

The places of those who were put out of Geneva were more than filled by those who came in from without, fleeing from persecution in France, Italy, Spain, Scotland and England. Six thousand came into a city where the number of people was normally thirteen thousand. Calvin nearly killed himself looking after them.

The stories of how some of these refugees made their escape from their native country have come down to us. There was, for example, Curio of Turin in Italy, who was thrown into prison there because of his Lutheran views. The door of the prison was open, but Curio's feet were in chains. After a day or so one foot began to swell and he suggested to the jailer that one chained foot would be enough to hold him. Might he not have the other free and change off to relieve the soreness? The jailer consented and for some time the chain was shifted every day from one leg to the other. Now Curio was dressed as were the men of that time in stockings as long as tights. He pulled off the stocking on the free leg, stuffed it with rubbish, and tucked his own leg under him. When the jailer came to shift the chain, Curio put the stuffed stocking in the padlock. The door was not watched and he was able to make an easy escape to Switzerland. Later he came back for his wife and children.

Caracciolo was a nobleman of Naples, thirty-five years old, happily married, and the father of six children. He came to believe in the views of Calvin, but his father and wife and children did not. He well knew that if he made known his faith he would lose his life and all his property would be taken away from his family. Caracciolo was in the service of the Emperor Charles V and by him was sent on government business to the north. Here he decided that he would not return but would go to Geneva and send word to his family to join him there. They, however, were no more willing to live in a Protestant country than was he to remain in a Catholic, and in fact they could not. Geneva would not permit Catholics any more than Naples would permit Protestants. The father, who was a relative of the Pope, tried to make arrangements whereby the family could be united at Venice, and each could follow his own religion, but the wife was unwilling to live with her husband unless he would return to the Church. Caracciolo felt that he must see her. A meeting was planned at a safe place but she did not come. He decided to risk his life by going home. At first his father and wife and children received him with joy, for they thought he had come home to stay. When they learned that he had come only to persuade them to join him, the father cursed, the wife wept, and the children begged him to stay, and the twelve-year-old girl took hold of his feet to keep him home. Yet he well knew that the only condition on which he could stay would be to change his religion and that he would not do. Back to the boat he went, while the family stood on the shore waving to him to stay. He became an elder in the Italian church at Geneva.

Theodore Beza was a French refugee. Here is a picture of him drawn by a schoolboy. The same boy did the picture of Calvin shown on a previous page. Beza's father was very much troubled because his son had left the Catholic Church and France, and begged for a chance to talk with him in the hope of bringing him back. A meeting was arranged at a safe point. Beza wrote to Calvin about it. "A hard struggle faces me with my father whom I am to meet in five days on the border. May God give me strength to stand up against the attacks upon my heart and to win my father if possible

for the Master. More than any threats I am afraid of his look, his tender pleas, the tears of my father, the old man. I hope that this time as in the past God will stand by me and that all may turn out to His glory."

John Knox was a refugee from Scotland. That country at the time was not yet united with England and was closely bound to France. The Queen was a French princess. When Protestantism began in the land, French Catholics were ready to interfere and Knox, being a Protestant preacher, was taken by the French and made a galley slave, that is, a rower in a sailing vessel. Such slaves were chained to the benches and whipped to make them pull harder. Once Knox had to row the ship past the shore on which he could see the spire of the church in which he used to preach. He wondered whether he would ever speak there again.

An exchange of prisoners brought his release, but he was not then able to return to Scotland. Instead he found his way to Geneva. Here he stayed and learned from Calvin until a door opened to win Scotland for the Reform. Knox came back just as Mary became the Queen of Scots. Her mother was French and Mary herself had been brought up in France and was strongly Catholic. Scotland, as we have said, was at that time a country separate from England. Knox wanted to unite them. But in those days they could not have been united if one were Catholic and the other Protestant. England had become Protestant. Either then England must go back to the Catholic Church or Scotland must become Protestant. Knox was determined that the latter should happen because he believed Protestantism to be the true form of the Church.

A conflict followed with the Queen. So long as she was a Catholic, Knox was not ready to obey her as queen. She called him in and asked whether he thought it right that subjects should disobey sovereigns. "Certainly," said he, "did not Daniel and the Apostles refuse to obey?" He told her that if a ruler expected obedience he or she must obey the true Church. "But the Kirk of Rome is the one I will obey," said she, and spoke of her conscience. Knox could not understand how she could have a conscience if she did not follow the Bible.

The contest grew bitter and ended in war. Mary lost the

throne. The country became Presbyterian. Her son James later became the King of the united countries of Scotland and England. No one did more than Knox to make the union possible by first uniting the two kingdoms in the Protestant faith.

Calvinism spread also into France and for a time seemed on the point of winning the day until wars of religion broke out— fierce wars in which no side showed mercy. Protestants wore strings of priests' ears and a Catholic commander asked his men: "Why do you crowd the prisons with Protestant captives? Is the river full?" Calvinists destroyed Catholic churches and smashed images and crucifixes. Catholics were responsible for the massacre of Saint Bartholomew in which many Calvinists lost their lives. The story is told of one man who escaped by hiding in a loft under some hay. The soldiers poked in their swords but just missed him. He hid there for several days, fed by a hen who laid an egg every day and did not cackle.

The wars so wrecked France that people became thoroughly sick of them and began to see that it would be better to have two religions and one country than one religion and no country. The leader of those who took this view was Henry of Navarre. His mother had trained him as a Protestant but when he went to school he was whipped every day for a month until he agreed to go to Mass. When through school he became a Protestant again. In the massacre of Saint Bartholomew he saved his life by going to Mass, and when the danger was over returned to the Huguenots. Henry became King as Henry IV, but the Catholics would not obey him unless he joined their Church. After many vain attempts to capture Paris by force, he decided the city was worth a Mass. But having become Catholic he granted freedom to the Huguenots in the Edict of Nantes of 1598.

CHAPTER SEVENTEEN

THE OPEN BIBLE

NGLAND, as we have seen, was already Protestant when Knox began his work in Scotland, leading to the union of the two countries. Now we shall see how England came first to be Protestant. Another conflict of Church and State had arisen in the country like those contests which had been frequent in the Middle Ages. The earlier struggles never had very serious results for the unity of the Church. The ruler would be excommunicated and the country interdicted, but in the end the ruler would yield or the Pope would soften his demands and Church and State would work together again. Perhaps the same thing would have happened this time in England if the Protestant Reformation had not already started in Germany and Switzerland.

The King of England was Henry VIII. He was married to a Spanish princess, Catherine of Aragon, and she was the aunt of the Holy Roman Emperor Charles V. All the children of Henry and Catherine died as babies except one and she was a girl, the Princess Mary. Henry was afraid that if he did not have a son to follow him on the throne when he died there might be a war as to who should be King. There had been such wars in England just before his time, the Wars of the Roses. He feared that if he had no son the wars might break out again. For that reason he asked the Pope to let him put away Catherine and take another wife. The Pope, of course, could not grant a divorce, but there had been a flaw in Henry's marriage which would make it possible to say that it had never been a proper marriage. The Pope might have been willing to say this had not the Emperor Charles V stepped in to stop Henry and the Pope from doing anything to his Aunt Catherine.

Henry thereupon took things into his own hands and separated the Church in England from the Church in Rome. The King himself was made the head of the English Church for the management of its outward affairs. The Archbishop of Canterbury became the head for religious matters. The new Church was called the Church of England. In America it is called the Episcopal Church. The word episcopal comes from the Greek for bishop and an episcopal church is one ruled by bishops. There are, therefore, many episcopal churches, but there is just one which calls itself the Episcopal Church.

In England it is called the Church of England. Just as the Western and the Eastern Churches separated because the Greeks and the Latins had drifted apart; just as the Protestant Reformation spread to the north rather than to the south, in part because the Germanic and the Latin peoples were different, so now a separated Church was formed in England because in this country a strong nation had grown up separate from Europe. The world of the Middle Ages was splitting up and the Church was divided at the same time.

Henry took advantage of the split to take money away from the Church. There had long been quarrels over money matters between Church and State. Now Henry saw his chance to shut down all of the monasteries and take all of their lands and buildings and income. Really the monasteries were not so useful as they once had been. In an earlier time they had been retreats from the barbarians, outposts for Christianizing and civilizing new countries, centers of learning and hospitality. But the Black Death of 1348 took the lives of so many people in England that there were not enough left of the right kind to fill up the ranks of the monks. The Catholic Church, itself, was closing down some of the monasteries. Henry went ahead with a high hand and closed them all, pretending to have caught the monks in wicked living.

The Church of England, however, was not very different from the Church of Rome. The majority of the English people still loved the Catholic Church, its sacraments and its services. In making changes Henry moved slowly. The man whom he chose as Archbishop of Canterbury was Thomas Cranmer. He shared some of Luther's ideas and he really believed that there had been a flaw in Henry's marriage. He was glad to see Henry break with the Pope and set up a separate Church. Just as the princes had helped to reform the Church in Germany and the town councils in Switzerland, so Cranmer believed the King had the right to reform the Church in England, and to be its head and to manage its outward affairs. Cranmer was willing, therefore, to go slowly so long as the King wished to go slowly.

The only important change at first was that the Bible in English rather than in the Latin language was placed in all the churches.

The translation chosen for the purpose had had a curious history. It was largely the work of William Tyndale who translated not from the Latin of Saint Jerome like Wyclif's helpers, but from the Greek Testament printed by Erasmus. Tyndale could not print his book in England because at that time Henry was hoping to get what he wanted from the Pope and was doing his best to please him. Henry even wrote a book against Martin Luther, and the Pope called Henry the Defender of the Faith. The words which mean this in Latin, *Defensor Fidei*, are still on the English coins (usually just D. F.), though the faith has changed. Henry at that time was so afraid of displeasing the Pope that he would not permit a translation made by a Protestant to be printed in England. The work was done in Germany and the books smuggled in. The English officials bought up as many copies as possible for burning and Tyndale got the money from the sales and used it to put out a better printing. After Henry broke with the Pope this book which had been bought up for burning was the very one placed by Archbishop Cranmer in all the churches.

Most of the English people accepted what Henry did. A few of the monks and churchmen and officials of the State believed that he as King had no right in any sense to be the head of the Church of Christ, nor had the English Parliament any right to make laws for the Church of Christ. Henry put to death those who would not submit.

Among them was the gallant Sir Thomas More, whom the Catholic Church has lately made a saint. When a friend told More that he should recognize the King as the head of the Church because Parliament said so, More answered, "Suppose Parliament should make a law that God should not be God? Would you then say that God were not God?" When he was being taken by the guard to be imprisoned in the Tower of London, his daughter dashed through the soldiers and threw her arms about his neck, saying only, "Oh, my Father! Oh, my Father!" In his last letter to her, he wrote, "I never liked your manner to me better than when you kissed me last, for I love it when daughterly love and dear charity hath no leisure to look to worldly courtesies." Wit and courage did not leave him at the end. To the officer at the scaffold he said, "See me safe up, I'll take care of myself coming down." "I die," he said, "loyal to God and to the King, but to God first of all."

Henry did marry another wife after putting Catherine away, but the second wife also had no son, only a daughter, the Princess Elizabeth. A third wife did have a son. His name was Edward. When Henry died this son followed him as Edward VI. He was only a boy of nine years. The real ruler of the country was his uncle and he was much more Protestant than Henry had been. Encouraged by that fact Protestants of the hotter sort began to write poems against the bishops of the Catholic Church and against the Pope and to urge that England as fast as possible should move away from the Church of Rome. Here is one of the poems. Of the bishops it is said:

Alack, for Christ's might,
These things go not aright;
Our lanterns give no light;
All bishops be not bright;
They be so full of spite,
They care not whom they bite;
Both friend and foe they smite
With prison, death, and flight;
So daily they do fight
To overturn the right;

So we be in the plight
That losing of our sight,
We know not black from white,
And be thus blinded quite,
We know not day from night.

Of the Pope they complained,

He robbeth all nations
With his fulminations,
And other like vexations;
As with abjurations,
Excommunications,
Aggravations,
Presentations,
Sequestrations,
Deprivations,
Advocations,
Resignations,
Dilapidations,
Sustentations,
Administrations,
Approbations,
Assignations,
Alterations,
Narrations,
Declarations,
Locations,
Collocations,
Revocations,
Dispensations,
Intimations,
Legitimations,
Insinuations,
Pronunciations,
Demonstrations,
Vacations,
Convocations,
Deputations,
Donations,
Condonations,
Excusations,
Declamations,
Visitations,
Acceptations,
Publications,
Renunciations,
False foundations,
And dissimulations,
With like abominations,
Of a thousand fashions.

While the people were being stirred up by such poems, the King's uncle went ahead and stopped the Catholic Mass. In its place, he ordered a service in accordance with the views of Luther and in the English language. Archbishop Cranmer was given the task of preparing a prayer book for the Church of England. He succeeded so well that the *Book of Common Prayer*, more than anything else, has endeared the English Church to the English people. The words to be said in serving the Lord's Supper were these: "The body of our Lord Jesus Christ, which was given for thee, preserve thy body and soul unto everlasting life. The blood of our Lord Jesus Christ, which was shed for thee, preserve thy body and soul unto everlasting life." These words would satisfy a Lutheran, and, possibly, even a Catholic. They suggest that Christ's body is really in the bread and in the wine. Strict Protestants, therefore, disliked these words and for their sake, Cranmer put out a second prayer book, in which the form was changed to read: "Take and eat this in remembrance that Christ died for thee, and feed on Him in thy heart by faith, with thanksgiving. Drink this in remembrance that Christ's blood was shed for thee, and be thankful." The word, "remembrance" suggests that the Lord's Supper is only a reminder of Christ's suffering, as Zwingli once had taught. "Feeding in the heart" was what Calvin believed.

Edward was a frail lad and died when he was fifteen. He was followed by his half-sister, the Princess Mary, and the war which Henry feared if a girl came after him never happened. England accepted Mary as Queen. She was the daughter of Catherine of Aragon and had never left the Catholic Church. Now she brought all England back to the Roman Church. Then the Protestants suffered as the Catholics had done under her father. The leading bishops were burned. When Bishops Ridley and Latimer were bound to stakes at Oxford, Latimer said to his friend, "Be of good cheer, Master Ridley, and play the man, for we shall this day light such a candle in England as I trust by God's grace shall never be put out."

Cranmer was in a very hard place. He believed in Luther's teaching. At the same time, he had said that the King of England might choose the form of religion. Henry and Edward had chosen Protestantism. That suited Cranmer very well. Now Mary was Queen and she chose to return to the Catholic Church. Cranmer decided that he must accept her decision and wrote his consent, then tore it up, for his conscience was at war with his reasoning. He did this several times, and in the end cursed Luther and Zwingli and himself for following them. Nevertheless, Cranmer was condemned to be burned and before his death he was required to stand in the church at Oxford and repeat his submission to the Queen and to the Pope. In the midst of this, Cranmer broke off. "Now I come," he said, "to that which troubles my conscience more than anything that I ever did or said in my whole life, and that is that through fear of death I signed with my hand what I do not believe in my heart. When I come to the fire, this hand shall be the first to burn." He went out smiling. When the fire leapt up, he held his right hand in the flame until it was burned away.

Mary, like her brother, ruled only five years and was followed by her half-sister, Princess Elizabeth. People by this time were weary of beheadings and burnings. Elizabeth wanted to be done with all this and to satisfy as many people as possible. Of course, she had to decide to be either Protestant or Catholic, and she did decide to be Protestant, but she tried to require from the people only those beliefs which would be least troublesome to Catholics and acceptable to all Protestants. In the Prayer Book, she simply put together the forms of Cranmer's first and second books.

Elizabeth, herself, would not tell any one what she did believe. She is said to have written this verse about the Lord's Supper:

> Christ was the word that spake it,
> He took the bread and brake it,
> And what His words do make it,
> That I believe and take it.

Here is an Elizabethan family at prayer.

SOLDIERS OF THE POPE

CATHOLIC reform, in the meantime, was not lagging and the Catholic Church was busy correcting many of the faults which had done so much to cause the Protestant Reformation. The efforts of mediæval reformers like Thomas à Kempis, Ximenes and Erasmus were continued by new orders of the Catholic Church founded to rekindle zeal and preserve the "Vray Foy." These words on the banner above mean in old French the "True Faith." This was the banner of a Scottish chieftain in the days when Scotland was still Catholic and in league with France. Among the new Catholic orders we shall look at three: the Capuchin, the Jesuit and the Daughters of Charity.

The Capuchins were a new branch of the Franciscans and arose in the year 1528. Their outward mark was a pointed cap, which they supposed was the kind actually worn by Saint Francis. Their inward mark was to follow in his footsteps, observing his poverty and caring for the poor and sick. When food was scarce, one brother would say to another, "Take it. You need it more than I."

177

The other would reply. "I am young and can go without it more easily." And the food would go uneaten, since neither would have it from the other. When plagues took the people, the Capuchins were the first to volunteer. They also became missionaries.

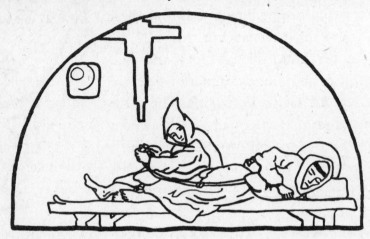

One of the greatest orders in reforming the Church, spreading the faith, and winning back lands which had gone over to the Protestants, was the Jesuits, meaning, the Order of Jesus. Their founder was a Spanish nobleman, Ignatius Loyola. He had been a knight, fighting for the Queen of Spain against the French. In the siege, a cannon ball struck him in the leg and left him upon the walls in a pool of blood. The French, on taking the town, treated him carefully, and took him to the Loyola Castle to get well. But the bone was badly set and the leg was not straight. Ignatius had it broken again and reset, and then again a second time. When a piece stuck out, he had it sawn off, and then the leg was too short and he had it pulled. Nothing would make it right. He could be a soldier no more.

As he lay upon his bed, he made up his mind instead of being a knight of the Queen of Spain to become a knight of the Queen

of Heaven, the Virgin Mary. Though a grown man, he went to
school with little boys and then to the university, that he might
know enough to be a teacher. Yet he did
not wait to finish his course before starting
at once to teach people how to improve their
lives. The Church authorities felt he
might be teaching wrong ideas and had
him put in prison, but examination showed
that he was all right. From Spain he went
to France and in Paris gathered about him
a group of students. He would do so much
for them that they could not refuse his
wishes. One student to whom Ignatius
loaned money ran away with it, but a year
later, when that student was sick in another town, Ignatius walked
over to take care of him.

Ignatius taught this little student group to spend time in thinking about themselves, about their wrongdoing and God's anger
and God's love. He made everything plain and simple, so that no
one could miss it. A plan for self-examination was set forth on
five fingers. Number one is marked "Give Thanks" and shows
a figure thanking God, the Father. Number two is "Ask for
Light" and shows some one kneeling before the dove, which
stands for God's spirit. Number three is "Look at Yourself." Here
the figure is before Christ with the whip of cords. Number four
is "Be Sorry." The man is kneeling before the altar and looking
up at Christ upon the cross. Number five is "Do Something" and
shows a knight with a sword about to kill a dragon. This plan is
illustrated on the next page.

Ignatius Loyola intended to do something and offered his services and those of his followers to the Pope as a new order. They

were permitted to form the Society of Jesus, from which they were called the Jesuits. They were to be teachers of Catholics, the converters of Protestants, and missionaries to the non-Christians.

The Jesuits knew no fears. When one of them was about to go

into Germany to win back the Lutherans, he was told by the Protestants that if he came he would be drowned in the Rhine. He answered, "It is as short to heaven by water as by land." The Jesuit missionary to India was Francis Xavier. He had been a happy-go-lucky student. Ignatius challenged him to a game of billiards on condition that if he lost he would go through the exercise of self-examination. He lost and that was how he happened to go as a missionary to the Portuguese capital in India. Here he found that the navigators had already built churches— gilded cathedrals, which the natives did attend, but afterwards they would go home to worship monkeys and elephants as before.

The Portuguese made no effort to teach them and were concerned only to build palaces in the midst of huts. Xavier went to the natives. One day he heard of the pearl fishers who eight years before had promised to become Christians if the Portuguese would drive off the Mohammedans. This was done and the promise was kept. The Portuguese reported to their king that twenty thousand souls had been saved, but a priest had never come near them since. Xavier went barefooted, ringing a bell, and calling, "Come here. I have good news."

Then he went to Japan and from there his hope was to reach China, but no foreigner was allowed to enter that land. He still hoped that some one would smuggle him in, and wrote to a friend, "If you get to China, you will find me there—either in prison or in Peking." Xavier, with one friend, had himself carried to a deserted island off the coast of Canton and bargained with a smuggler to take him to the city for twenty hundredweight of pepper, but the smuggler took the pepper and never came back. Xavier sat looking in silence at the great heathen land waiting to be won for Christ, till death took him before he could find a way to enter.

The Daughters of Charity owed their foundation to Saint Vincent de Paul. His interest in the poor, in prisoners, slaves and the sick was awakened when he himself from rich and well became poor, sick, imprisoned and enslaved. He was a wealthy young man in France when one day he set sail from the French port of Marseilles. He tells us himself what happened: "The wind was good and we could have made Narbonne that day had not three Turkish ships swooped down upon us.

In the fight I received an arrow wound the scar of which I carry to this day. The pirates took our ships, butchered the captain and put the rest of us in irons. We were taken to Tunis and in chains were put up for sale as slaves. Merchants came to look us over as if we were horses or oxen. They made us open our mouths to see our teeth, felt our sides, made us walk, trot, run, carry weights and fight."

Vincent was bought first by a fisherman who found him no good at sea and sold him again. He came at length into the hands of a Frenchman who had been a friar of Saint Francis, but on being captured had won freedom by giving up his faith. He was now a well-to-do Mohammedan farmer. Vincent, as his slave, had to till the soil in the broiling sun. The master's wife was interested to find out about the slave's religion and told him to sing the praises of his God. He sang to her from the one hundred and thirty-seventh psalm, the words of the children of Israel when they were slaves in Babylon, "They that carried us away captive required of us a song; and they that wasted us required of us mirth, saying, Sing us one of the songs of Zion. How shall we sing the Lord's song in a strange land?" The woman was so moved that she told her husband he had done wrong to give up his faith. His conscience was touched and with Vincent he planned to escape. Ten months later their chance came and in a little boat they crossed the sea to France.

From that time forward Vincent decided to spend his life trying to help those in France who were suffering what he had suffered in Tunis. The French ships were rowed by galley slaves. You recall that John Knox had been one. Vincent sought out the general in charge of the galleys and persuaded him to let something be done for the men. For prisoners, too, Vincent was active.

Even greater labors were spent on the sick. The hospitals of those days were frightful. Those who were slightly sick were put with those on the point of death. The foul air and filth were enough to kill the most healthy. Saint Vincent—and he deserves from now on the title which the Church has given him—enlisted young women to serve as nurses. They did not become regular nuns. They took no vows to spend all their lives at this work. At first they had no special dress, though now they wear a starched headpiece. They were to live simply, dress plainly and give all their strength to the sick and poor for as long as they were willing. "Your monasteries," the Saint told them, "are houses of the sick. Your cell is a hired room; your chapel the parish church; your cloister the streets of the city; your walled-in dwelling is simply obedience; the gate that guards you is the fear of God; your veil is modesty."

The sisters loved their work and would not give it up for easy living. Once a duchess, hearing of these nurses, desired that one should come to live with her as a companion. When one of the Daughters of Charity was asked to go she answered, "I left my father and mother to serve the poor and I cannot serve this noble-woman." Another daughter was persuaded to go but was promised that she might come back in five days if she wished. The duchess said to her, "My child, are you not content to stay with me?"

"Madame," she answered, "I left my father's house to serve the poor. If you were poor I would gladly stay."

At the end of five days she was back in the hospital.

The Papacy in our time has become somewhat different from what it was in the Middle Ages. Many of the conflicts of Church and State happened then because the Papacy was itself a state with lands of its own and even with armies of its own. This arrangement was especially bad for Italy because it meant that she could never have one government for the whole country so long as the Church was itself a government for a part of the country. In the year 1870 Italy was made one nation and all power as a state was taken away from the Church.

The popes disliked this very much because they said that the Head of the Church ought not to have to live in the country of any earthly ruler because the Church speaks for the Heavenly Ruler of all men. The difficulty was solved in 1929 when the Pope was permitted to be the ruler of a very tiny piece of land in Rome called the Vatican City. It is not big enough to hurt the unity of Italy, but it is large enough to remove the Pope from the rulership of any earthly king. The Pope has his own railway station, his own radio from which he can speak to all the world, and his own postage stamp. One of these appears below showing the church of St. Peter.

The popes in recent years have worked hard for the peace of the world. Pope Pius XI at the close of the first World War said that hatred between nations hurts even those who have won a war and makes trouble for the future. "We must not forget," said he, "that the best way to keep peace is not by a forest of bayonets but by trust in one another and friendship."

CHAPTER NINETEEN

BACK TO THE BIBLE

N spite of the efforts of the Catholic Church to mend its faults the breach between Catholic and Protestant grew wider and wider in the days of Queen Elizabeth. This was the time of the wars of religion and of the massacre of Saint Bartholomew in France, a time when the Calvinists and the Jesuits plotted against the lives of the rulers of the opposite faith. A cartoonist who was sick of such quarrels pictured Luther, Calvin and the Pope pulling each other's beards and ears as shown on the next page. In England Queen Elizabeth was excommunicated by the Pope and her Catholic subjects were told that they need not obey her as Queen. Plots were on foot to take her life and place upon her throne Mary Queen of Scots who, having fled from Scotland, was a prisoner in England. Because of these plots Mary was beheaded and Catholics came to be feared and hated. The cry arose of "No Popery."

The feeling became still stronger when Elizabeth was followed by James, the son of Mary Queen of Scots. Under him Scotland

and England were united. He was James VI of Scotland and James I of England. Some thought he might be well disposed to the Catholics because his mother had been a Catholic. Others thought he would be a Presbyterian because he had been brought up by the Presbyterians in Scotland. He disappointed them both and took his stand for the Church of England of which as King he was the head. Then the Catholics plotted against him and an

attempt was made to blow up the House of Parliament. The folly of hotheads enraged all England against all Catholics.

But little was done to Catholics in England because they were few. The rage of Englishmen vented itself rather on anything in the Church of England which resembled the Church of Rome. The Church of England must be purified, was the cry. The people who wanted to do it were called Puritans.

They were not altogether of one mind as to what needed to be purified. Some saw the model in the Presbyterian Church in Scotland. Others looked to the Reformed Church of Zwingli. Still others felt that no Church as yet had reached the perfect pattern of the Bible. Objection was common to certain practices of the Church of England which were supposed to have come from the Church of Rome, such as the use of a ring at weddings, kneeling before the altar at the Lord's Supper, making with the fingers the sign of the cross over one baptized, the wearing of a vestment or special dress by the clergy, the placing of organs in churches and crosses on steeples. Some disliked the *Book of Common Prayer* on the ground that prayers should come straight from the heart instead of being written out.

The Puritans tried to persuade Parliament to alter the forms of the Church of England. When Parliament did nothing, some Puritans consented to remain in the Church of England, and continued to make disturbances from within. Others left and started churches of their own on the outside. They were variously known as Separatists, Non-Conformists, Dissenters and Independents. The principal ones were the Presbyterians, Congregationalists, Baptists, Quakers and Unitarians. The Presbyterians we have already noticed in Scotland. The Unitarians will come in the next chapter. The Congregationalists, Baptists and Quakers will be in this chapter.

The struggle between the Puritans and the Church of England was well under way at the end of the reign of Queen Elizabeth. She called them "fault finders" and managed to keep things somewhat quiet. Hopes were high that King James would bring Presbyterianism from Scotland to England, but he had found out that a presbytery "agreeth as well with kingship as God and the devil." All that he would do for the Puritans was to consent to have a better translation made of the Bible. It is called the King James Version. For stateliness of language there is nothing finer in the English tongue.

All the other desires of the Puritans James refused, and he had the ill luck to stir them up at an unexpected point. The King put out a "Book of Sports" to be played on Sundays after church. "Not to allow such sports," said the King, "will prevent Catholics from becoming Protestants when they see that no honest mirth or recreation is lawful or tolerable in Our Religion, which cannot but breed a great discontentment in Our people's hearts, especially

of such as are, peradventure, upon the point of turning; the other
inconvenience is, that this prohibition barreth the common and
meaner sort of people from using such exercises as may make
their bodies more able for war, when we, or our successors, shall
have occasion to use them. And, in place thereof, sets up filthy
tipplings and drunkenness, and breeds a number of idle and discontented speeches in their ale houses. For when shall the common
people have leave to exercise, if not upon the Sundays and holy
days, seeing they must apply their labor, and win their living
in all working days?"

But the Puritans would have none of it. Their idea of the true
and false keeping of Sunday is shown in these two contrasting
pictures. They had been studying the King James Bible in which
they read, "Remember the Sabbath day, to keep it holy." Another
reason was that the Puritans did not have religious services every
day of the week as Calvin had done in Geneva. So many services
interfered too much with work, but if Sunday was to be the only
religious day, it must be given to religion and to nothing else.
"Of course," said one of the Puritans, "the Bible says that if the
ox or the ass fall into the pit on the Sabbath day, you may pull

them out, but do not push them in on Saturday in order that they may be there to be pulled out on Sunday." The Westminster catechism of the Presbyterians (a catechism is a book of questions and answers for children to learn about religion) says in question 60: "How is the Sabbath to be sanctified? Answer: The Sabbath is to be sanctified by a holy resting all that day, even from such worldly employments and recreations as are lawful on other days and by spending the time in public and private exercises of God's worship, except so much as is to be taken up in works of necessity and mercy." The Puritans would have nothing to do with James' "Book of Sports."

Charles the First, the son of James, was unwise enough to put out a new printing of the "Book of Sports." He irritated the Puritans still more by marrying a French princess who was a Catholic. The Puritans grew ever more extreme. Some objected to Christmas because it ends in "mas" which is nothing more nor less than the Catholic Mass. Observance of Christmas among the Dissenters disappeared for about two hundred years. Then the Prayer Book and the dress of the clergy became more and more objects of attack. The brunt of the blows fell upon Archbishop Laud. He was willing to let people believe much as they liked, provided they would worship and dress in the same way in church. Since the Church was the Church of England, all England must pray in the same way and all England meant Scotland, too, since the countries had been united under James. But the Scotch were Presbyterians. When Laud commanded that the Prayer

Book be used in the Scotch churches, and when a minister did use it in Edinburgh, a woman in the audience flung her stool at his head. Worse than that happened to heads in England. Three Puritans for their hot words against Laud lost their ears. Many heads were put behind bars like the one at the beginning of this chapter. Laud in turn lost his head. Here is a Puritan cartoon which shows

him standing on the Tower of London looking down at the gallows awaiting him.

War broke out. The Scotch joined with the English Parliament against King Charles both over religious and other matters. Oliver Cromwell took the lead. The King was beheaded. Cromwell became Lord Protector. This was the day when the Puritans were in power. The use of the Prayer Book was stopped. The Westminster Assembly met and drew up the Westminster Confession and the Westminster Catechism used by the Presbyterian Churches. The "Book of Sports" was burned, and in the cathedrals the stained glass windows having pictures of Catholic saints were smashed. One Puritan tells how he took a fifty-foot ladder in Canterbury Cathedral and climbing up with a hammer sent Saint Thomas à Becket's glassy bones clattering to the ground. Worst of all, Catholics were persecuted in Ireland.

The English wearied of Puritan extremes and, after Cromwell, welcomed back Charles II and the Church of England. Then severe measures were taken against Non-Conformists. Charles II was followed by his brother James II, a Catholic. The English put him out and called over from Holland William and Mary. This was in 1689. An edict of toleration granted freedom of religion to all groups except the Catholics. The laws against them lasted until 1829, and petty annoyances of the Dissenters lasted until the beginning of the present century.

During the time of the turmoil arose the Dissenters, such as the Congregationalists, Baptists, and Quakers. The Congregationalists were founded by a man named Robert Browne. For that reason they were called Brownists, but they did not like the name because Browne, after being in prison thirty-two times, grew tired and went back to the Church of England. In his Congregational days he complained of the majority of the Puritans because they stayed in the Church of England and waited for Parliament to start a reform. Browne wrote a booklet called *A Treatise on Reform without Tarrying for Any*. The Congregationalists began worshipping in their own way in the fields. Spies would watch them and report them to the government. Congregationalists went even further than other Puritans in getting away from everything Catholic. Some claimed that cathedrals where the Mass had once been observed were temples of Antichrist, and barns would do just as well for churches. Some said that pulpits were nothing but tubs. Their opponents pictured them preaching in tubs. Crosses on churches and bells and organs also must go. One man even objected to hymn books on

the ground that singing should be from the heart and not from a book. After a while these extreme points were forgotten. Bells and organs and pulpits and cathedrals came back, but not crosses on steeples. Of course, all of these points are not very important. The essential Congregational teaching was that the Church should be governed not by bishops nor by presbyteries, but by congregations. Here is a cartoon against the Congregationalists which shows them using a room in an inn for a church and a tub for a pulpit.

Some of the Congregationalists fled from England to Holland.

They had great difficulty in getting away, because all goods were required to be examined by the customs officials before any one could leave. The fugitives were afraid to let the officers know they were leaving for fear of being put in jail. Instead they tried to slip away and take passage with a Dutch captain. The men walked overland to the meeting place. Rowboats took the goods and the women and children along the coast. By the time they reached the Dutch ship, the women and children were already seasick, but the men, having walked, were all right. The captain decided to let the women have a little rest on shore and to take on the men first. He had just done so when the customs officers appeared over the hills, whereupon the captain sailed off with the men, leaving the women and children. They were taken by the officers from court to court and only with great difficulty and in little parties were able in the end to join their husbands and fathers in Holland.

There the English learned to know the Mennonites, who, as we have seen, taught that babies should not be baptized. Some of the English came to agree with them. In this way the English Baptist Church was founded. Helwys, the leader, later returned to England and spread Baptist teachings. In other respects the Baptists agreed with the Congregationalists. The Baptists were the first to state in their belief that men should not be forced to worship contrary to conscience. "Men should choose their religion themselves, seeing that they only must stand themselves before the judgment seat of God to answer for themselves."

One of the great Baptists of Charles the Second's day was John Bunyan. As a young man, he had played games on Sunday afternoon. He was worried because he knew the Puritan teaching. In the midst of a game he thought to himself, "Will you stop and be saved, or will you go on and be damned?" Then he thought that since he was damned anyway, he might as well finish the game. In his *Country Rhymes for Children* he wrote:

> An egg is not a chicken by falling from a hen,
> Nor is a man a Christian, till he is born again.

Bunyan was born again. Something happened to make him on fire for God. He had to tell everybody. On the following page he is shown preaching in the village square. Such gatherings outside of the churches, the laws of Charles the Second did not permit. Bunyan was thrown into jail and threatened with being sent out of the country and being hanged if he came back. The officer, named Cobb, was a friendly man, and came to the prison and tried to persuade Bunyan to change his mind.

"Why cannot you give up public meetings?" asked Cobb. "The law does not stop you from talking to people one by one."

"If I may talk to one, why not to two?" asked Bunyan. "And if to two, why not to three? And if to three, why not to four? And we shall soon have a meeting."

"If they send you to Constantinople, you won't be able to preach to anybody," Cobb reminded him, and then went on to tell him that he should obey the government as Paul said.

"Yes," answered Bunyan, "but Paul was put in prison. There is more than one way to obey. We can obey by doing everything we are told and we can obey by refusing and suffering what is done to us."

"At this," writes Bunyan, "Cobb sat still and said no more. I thanked him for his civil and meek discourse with me, and so we parted. Oh, that we might meet in heaven."

Bunyan lay in prison and as he lay he dreamed a dream. The dream was the *Pilgrim's Progress*, the book most widely read by children in early America. In this book is a song which with some changes has been made into a hymn. The words as Bunyan wrote them are these:

> Who would true valor see,
> Let him come hither.
> One here will constant be
> Come wind, come weather.
> There's no discouragement
> Shall make him once relent
> His first avowed intent
> To be a Pilgrim.
>
> Who so beset him round
> With dismal stories,
> Do but themselves confound;
> His strength the more is.
> No lion can him fright,
> He'll with a giant fight,
> But he will have a right
> To be a Pilgrim.

The Quakers or Friends were started by George Fox. He, too, like the Puritans, wanted to give up everything that had been added to the Bible by the Catholics. He decided that the names of the days and months had been added from the names of heathen gods. In the Bible we do not hear about March, which comes from Mars, the God of War; nor about Sunday, the Sun's day; Monday, the Moon's day; nor of Wednesday, the day of Woden, the Norse God; or Saturday, from Saturn, the Roman God. The Quakers say simply, "first day, second day; first month, second month." Fox found a great following among people who called themselves "Seekers," because they were seeking for light.

Fox got into great trouble because he would not take off his hat. In those days men took off their hats not only to women, but to all those in authority, and even to each other, and made great bowings and scrapings. Fox thought such silly politeness should be stopped. When brought into court and asked where it says in the Bible to keep hats on, he answered, "Shadrach, Meshach, and Abednego went into the fiery furnace with their hose and their coats and their hats on."

The Quakers, like the Anabaptists, objected to oaths and war. Fox was often brought into court for refusing an oath. He would be given the Bible and told to swear by it. "Shall I swear," asked he, "by the book which says 'Swear not at all'?"

The Quakers gave up all the sacraments—even baptism and the Lord's Supper, because they say, "We need nothing outward to bring us to God." They gave up not only pulpits, but also ministers. In Quaker meetings, all sit in silence—men, women, and children —and wait quietly until God's spirit moves the hearts of all and perhaps leads some one to speak.

Women speak in Quaker meetings as well as men. This practice at first seemed dreadful to the other Churches, because Paul said that women should not speak in church. Here is a cartoon against the Quakers, showing a woman preaching on a tub. The Quakers gave to women a new place. None did more than the

Quakers for the improvement of prisons. They knew what they were like. Fox had spent many years in prisons all over England, so had other Quakers. Conditions were terrible. Men and women, sick and well, were herded together in unspeakable filth. When the Quakers got out, they did their best to have prisons changed.

Once when George Fox was in prison, the governor told him that if there were any disturbances among the people, he would be hanged over the wall. Fox answered, "I am ready for it. I have never feared death nor suffering in my life. I am an innocent, peaceable man, free from all plots and uprisings. I have always sought the good of all men. Bring out your gallows." The officers said, "He is as stiff as a tree and as pure as a bell."

The Quakers often claimed that God would punish wicked England. Some may have wondered whether their words had not come true when London burned. The fire raged along a front of half a mile. The poor folk snatched up what few things they could carry and rushed to St. Paul's Church, which had walls of stone and was somewhat removed from the neighboring houses, but the wooden tower caught fire. This is the tower which stands out against the flames in the picture. Soon the stones were falling out of the walls, and the lead on the drains melted and ran down into the streets. The fire continued for four days and four nights and when it died down, three hundred and seventy acres had been

burned over. Thirteen thousand houses were destroyed and eighty-four churches, including St. Paul's.

A new London was to rise from the ashes and the man who did the most to plan the new city was Sir Christopher Wren. For the smaller churches he used a style of building which in a way copied a Greek temple and a Gothic cathedral. The body of the building was like the temple with columns in front. From the roof rose a tall Gothic spire. For the new St. Paul's Cathedral, however, he used the style of St. Peter's at Rome with a great dome, of which a picture was shown on the Vatican stamp on p. 184. London Cathedral was thirty-five years in building. When Wren was seventy-eight, he stood by as his son placed the last stone upon the crown.

These verses were recently written about the great architect:

Clever men
Like Christopher Wren
Only occur just now and then;
Never a cleverer dipped his pen,
Than clever Sir Christopher—
Christopher Wren.
With his chaste designs
On classical lines
His elegant curves and neat inclines,
And never an hour went by but when
London needed Sir Christopher Wren.
        "Salisbury Square
        Decidedly bare,
        Can you put one of your churches there?"
        London calling
        From ten to ten
        London calling
        Christopher Wren.*

[*Abridged from poem in *Kings—and Others Things* by Hugh Chesterman, published by Methuen.]

CHAPTER
TWENTY

THE AGE OF REASON

REEDOM in religion came with the eighteenth century. Then men had a chance to think and speak more calmly about the different kinds of religion, as to which of them was best or for that matter how far any of them might be true. The men of that age came to think that no one religion was best but the best was what all religions had in common, something simple and reasonable which everybody could understand and on which every one could agree. All the quarrels of the past, they said, arose from trying to make people believe too much. Christianity started out very simple and then grew complicated with doctrines like that of the Trinity. All that really matters, they said, is to believe that God made and created the world and sent His Son to teach and help the world. Men should be kind to each other, that is all. Everything else is superstition which the enlightened mind—the period is called the Enlightenment—could not believe and did not need to believe. All of the Churches adopted some of these ideas in the eighteenth century, and especially the Unitarians.

As for all the teaching about hell and devils and witches in which religious people had believed until then, this is all a bad fairy tale, said the Enlightenment. There is no such place as hell and there are no such things as devils and witches. To treat crazy people as if they had devils is unkind and untrue. In the Middle Ages people supposed that insane persons actually had devils inside them. The treatment was to have the priest say holy words which would cast out the devil, as in this picture. Catholics and Protestants alike in the sixteenth and seventeenth centuries still believed that crazy or even queer persons were witches, who made friends with devils, brewed in cauldrons mixtures of toads, serpents, poison herbs and all things nasty. Witches rode broomsticks in the air and worshipped a god with a head of a goat. They were supposed to bring curses and plagues on the earth. Sometimes harmless and helpless old women, sometimes men in high positions, were accused by enemies of practising witchcraft and were burned. The Enlightenment ended all that.

Those who started the movement hoped to make Christianity stronger by stripping it of those teachings which had caused wars and persecutions as well as of those beliefs which scientists found hard to accept. This was the age of science when the public mind was catching up with past discoveries like those of Copernicus who put the sun and not the earth at the center of the heavenly bodies, and with the new discoveries of Newton about the law of gravitation. All the universe seemed to be run in accord with divine rules. The God of Christianity is the one who made the

rules and reason in man is able to understand them. The poet
Addison wrote a poem about God's rule as seen by the reason of
man in the control of the heavenly bodies.

> The spacious firmament on high,
>   With all the blue ethereal sky,
> And spangled heavens, a shining frame,
>   Their great Original proclaim.
>
> The unwearied sun from day to day
>   Does his Creator's power display,
> And publishes to every land
>   The work of an almighty Hand.
>
> Soon as the evening shades prevail,
>   The moon takes up the wondrous tale,
> And nightly to the listening earth
>   Repeats the story of her birth;
>
> Whilst all the stars that round her burn,
>   And all the planets in their turn,
> Confirm the tidings as they roll,
>   And spread the truth from pole to pole.
>
> What though in solemn silence all
>   Move round this dark terrestrial ball;
> What though no real voice nor sound
>   Amidst their radiant orbs be found;
>
> In reason's ear they all rejoice,
>   And utter forth a glorious voice;
> For ever singing, as they shine,
>   "The Hand that made us is divine."

The pruning away of superstitions in Christianity began in the hope of making the tree healthy and stronger, but the cutting of one branch led to another. If God is a God of law who made the rules of the world and keeps them Himself, what are we to think of miracles in the Bible? Did God break His own rules by having Jesus walk on water and turn water into wine? The common answer was that God does not break the rules any more. He did break them just once in order to prove that Jesus was His Son. The historian Gibbon, however, pointed out that according to the Catholic Church God still breaks the rules. Miracles are supposed never to have stopped. Protestants deny Catholic miracles and usually say that no miracles occur today. But at what point, inquired Gibbon, did they then come to an end? The stories about miracles have never stopped. If the miracles stopped but the stories went on, the stories must be false and if the stories are false now, what reason have we to believe that they were true then? Of course they might have been true and God might have broken His laws once and have kept them ever after, but how do we know that He did? We have only old books to prove it and perhaps they are not trustworthy. Here is a cartoon of Gibbon outweighing a bishop.

Gibbon did no more than hint his doubts. Others became bolder. Tom Paine, who helped to stir up the American Revolution by  his book *Common Sense*, wrote another tract called *The Age of Reason*, in which he said that if the devil really took Jesus to the top of a high mountain from which he could see *all* the kingdoms of the earth, he ought to have discovered America. Others pointed out places in the Bible which do not agree. One doubt led to another until some wondered whether Jesus ever lived at all and whether the whole story of his life might not be made up. Bishop Whately of the Episcopal Church wrote a very clever answer, in which he took the arguments commonly used to prove that Jesus might never have lived to show that by the same line of reasoning Napoleon Bonaparte was not alive at that very time, although everybody well knew that he was then the Emperor of France and the terror of England. But how does everybody know? asked Whately. Napoleon is taken for granted. But nothing should be taken for granted. His story is so amazing that it sounds like a fairy tale. He is said to have risen from a corporal to an emperor. He led an army to Egypt and lost it. Nevertheless he was able to return to Europe and raise another army, with which he overran Europe until defeated in Russia. Then he came back and raised another army. Defeated at Leipzig, he raised another army. Imprisoned at Elba, he broke loose and raised another army. Everything told about him is so big as to suggest that the whole tale has been made up.

Whately imagined all that would be said in favor of believing that Napoleon was a real person.

The Objector would say: British soldiers had been wounded fighting him.
Reply: British soldiers have been wounded fighting some one, but how do they know it is Napoleon?
Objection: The newspapers tell about him.
Reply: How do the newspapers know?
Objection: Are we to suppose that the newspapers are all lying?
Reply: No, not all. One may be lying and the others may be fooled.
Objection: Why should any newspaper wish to make up such a story?
Reply: Simple enough, to raise the taxes. If the English people believe there is a real Napoleon in France who seeks to destroy their country,

they will be willing to pay more money for the army and navy and the government will get the money.

Objection: But Napoleon was seen in a cocked hat and a uniform standing on a ship off the coast of Plymouth.

Reply: To be sure somebody was seen in a cocked hat and a uniform standing on a ship off the coast of Plymouth, but who was close enough to know who was in the cocked hat and uniform?

Just after the appearance of Whately's tract the newspapers came out with the news that Napoleon was dead. "See," said Whately, "I killed him. They were afraid I was going to puncture their story. They have saved themselves by saying he is dead instead of admitting that he never was alive."

Whately certainly showed that although we should try to find out whether the Bible is true, we ought not to be more unbelieving about the Bible than we are about something which happens in our own day. Of course we cannot believe everything the newspapers tell us now, but if we refuse to believe anything they say we shall not find the truth either. To discover the truth we must be ready to inquire, sift, trust, and try to understand. Tom Paine's question about the mountain from which America might have been discovered really does not call for a serious answer. Jesus told the disciples about the temptations in story form and they never supposed that he had been on a real mountain. With regard to walking on the water or turning water into wine, God might indeed have made an exception to His ordinary rules, but we do need more than ordinary proof in order to believe that something so unusual actually happened. But if we go to the other extreme and refuse to believe anything which we have not seen ourselves, we shall have to give up not only everything before our time, but most of that which is happening now.

One fruit of the discussion was the growing sense that after all miracles such as walking on water, even if true, do not mean so much for us as the greater miracle of the life and death of Jesus. He was himself a miracle, whether or no he did the wonders told about him, and the greatest miracle that can happen to us is that we should be like him.

The Enlightenment saw that people cannot be enlightened if they are ignorant and religion itself needs to be taught and explained. Something of religion we may know because of the teaching of God's Spirit in our hearts, but the teaching of the Bible cannot be known unless we study and are taught what is in the book. In order to teach children the truths of religion and of the Bible Sunday Schools were started at the close of the eighteenth century. The Bible was printed especially for children partly in picture writing as in this verse. "And now also the

 is laid unto the root of the trees: every  there-

fore which bringeth not forth good ," and so on.

Hymns for children were written by Isaac Watts and others. Here are some examples:

> Let dogs delight to bark and bite,
>   For God hath made them so;
> Let bears and lions growl and fight,
>   For 'tis their nature to.
>
> But children, you should never let
>   Such angry passions rise;
> Your little hands were never made
>   To tear each other's eyes.

And again:

> Angels are happy clothed with wings,
> But our new clothes are dangerous things.
> The child well dressed had need beware
> Lest his fine raiment prove a snare.

Rather better was this rhyming version of the Ten Commandments.

1 Thou shalt have no more Gods than me,
2 Before no Idol bow thy Knee;
3 Take not the name of God in vain:
4 Nor dare the Sabbath-day profane.
5 Give both thy Parents Honor due.
6 Take heed that thou no Murder do.
7 Abstain from Words and Deeds unclean,
8 Nor steal, tho' thou art poor and mean,
9 Nor make a wilful Lie, nor love it.
10 What is thy Neighbour's dare not covet.

June 6 - 1762

Mary Harte

TWICE-BORN MEN

AN is like a clumsy juggler who cannot keep half a dozen balls in the air at once. Now one falls to the ground and now another. The Enlightenment kept in the air the balls of truth and learning and let fall the balls of zeal and power. In all the arguing about whether the Christian religion is true the greatest argument was forgotten, namely what the Christian religion can do. Still worse, there were many clergymen in the Church of England who did not care whether Christianity is true or what it can do. They were interested only in living comfortably at the Church's expense and increasing their incomes by taking the money from several churches at once. On the next page is a cartoon of a vicar spreading himself out with hands and feet on four churches. The actual care of these churches was left to poor curates, while the rich vicars enjoyed foxhunting and trips to Italy, or chatted with the neighboring landlords about pigs and horses.

If the churches were neglected and little was done for those who came to them, nothing whatever was done for those who stayed away from church. The masses of the English poor were too dirty and drunken to be welcomed by clean nice folk who drove in their carriages to church. Few thought of bringing religion to the poor of England.

Several revivals came in the last half of the eighteenth and the first half of the nineteenth centuries (roughly 1750 to 1850). We shall note three: Methodism, led by John Wesley and George Whitefield; Anglo-Catholicism, led by John Henry Newman; and the Salvation Army, led by General William Booth.

The Methodist movement was begun by a group of students at Oxford University, among them John Wesley and George Whitefield. They were called Methodists in scorn by their fellow students because they mapped out what to do with every minute of the day with so much *method*; so much time should be given to study, so much to prayer; so much to work with prisoners in the jails and so on. But even this "method" in religion which seemed too much to scoffers did not seem enough to John Wesley. He was *doing* enough, but he did not *feel* sure enough and warm enough.

At a quarter before nine in the evening on the 24th day of May of the year 1738 the feeling of certainty came to him. He could not doubt it now. He felt as if he really were born again. What happens, he said, when we are born the first time? We were alive before we were born, but we did not breathe as yet. Even so, although we may be alive in religion, we are not born until we begin to breathe the Spirit of God. The new birth is "the change wrought in the soul by the spirit of God when the love of the world is changed into the love of God, pride into humility, passion into meekness; hatred, envy, malice into sincere, tender, disinterested love for all mankind. In a word, it is that change whereby the earthy is turned into the mind which was in Christ Jesus. This is the nature of the new birth. So is every one that is born of the Spirit."

John Wesley wanted other people to have this feeling too. Whitefield had it. They had both become ministers of the Church of England and began preaching in the churches about the new birth, but the religious life of the Church had grown so cold that the members were blistered by the heat of this preaching and closed the pulpits to the Methodists. What then? "If the churches are closed, we will preach out of doors," said Whitefield and Wesley. They went to the people where they were, at the mouths of the coal pits as the miners went down or came up from work, to the villages of England and Scotland, Ireland and America.

The common people heard them gladly, and sometimes the audiences were as many as twenty and thirty thousand. But hoodlums tried to break up the meetings, by blowing horns, ringing bells, or hiring the town crier to bawl in front of the preacher. Sometimes cattle were driven into the congregation. Once a mob burst into the house where Wesley was staying. He walked into the thickest of them and called for a chair. "My heart was filled with love," he writes, "my eyes with tears, and my mouth with arguments. . . . They were amazed, they were ashamed, they melted down, they devoured every word. What a turn was this!" Wesley thanked God for getting together such a congregation of drunkards, swearers, and Sabbath breakers.

Sometimes the bullies got caught in their own traps. Once a man in the crowd lifted his hand to throw a stone when another thrown from behind caught him right between the fingers. Another came with pockets full of rotten eggs. Wesley writes, "A young man coming unawares clapped his hands on each side, and mashed them all at once." And sometimes the bullies were themselves overcome by the man they were trying to crush. When a mob was nearly on the point of killing Wesley and a stout club had

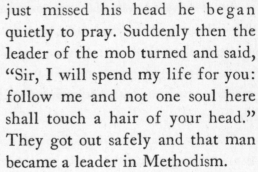

just missed his head he began quietly to pray. Suddenly then the leader of the mob turned and said, "Sir, I will spend my life for you: follow me and not one soul here shall touch a hair of your head." They got out safely and that man became a leader in Methodism.

Wesley rode up and down England, Scotland, Wales, and Ireland, preaching in the fields and visiting the jails. He always travelled on horseback. In seven months he covered 2400 miles and during his life 225,000 miles. Sometimes he made ninety miles in one day. He rode with a loose rein—that was the best way, he said, to keep a horse from stumbling, and as he rode he read: history, poetry, philosophy, in English, Latin and in Greek.

By and by the tide turned and people began to admire him. Mayors offered him the freedom of the cities in which he had been mobbed. In his eighty-fifth year on visiting a certain town he wrote: "The last time I was here, about forty years ago, I was taken prisoner by an immense mob, gaping and roaring like lions: but how is the tide turned! High and low now lined the street, from one end of the town to the other, out of stark love and kindness, gaping and staring as if the king were going by."

But this did not please Wesley so much as did the change in the people. Of one town he wrote that it had been "remarkable for Sabbath-breaking, cursing, swearing, drunkenness, and a general contempt of religion. But it is not so now." And again, "So is the roughest town become one of the quietest towns in England. . . . I will show you him that was a lion till then, and is now a lamb; him that was a drunkard and is now sober. . . . These are my living arguments for what I say, that God does now, as of old, forgive sins and send the Holy Spirit to us and to our children."

Wesley well knew that to stay this way men needed more help than mere preaching. For one who had been given to drink to keep sober was no easy matter. Old friends would tease him into taking one pint and then another until they had the fun of seeing a Methodist drunk. That this should not happen Methodists bound themselves together in classes of twelve members who met once a week to strengthen each other by telling the trials they had met, the struggles and the victories. Each member of the class had a ticket. At the head of this chapter is shown the ticket of "Mary Harte."

The movement grew. A building for meetings was secured in London. It had been a cannon factory the roof of which had been blown off. Wesley replaced the roof and turned it into a church. Men, who were not ordained ministers of the Church of England, as were Wesley and Whitefield, began preaching in this church. At first Wesley was inclined to stop them, but when he saw the power with which they preached he let them go on. The Methodists thus came to have "lay preachers." By and by more ordained ministers were needed and no bishop of the Church of England would ordain them. Thereupon Wesley himself set aside one who should ordain others. In this way the Methodist Church came to have bishops of its own. All of these steps, the class meetings, the church building, the lay preachers and the bishops made Methodism into a Church separate from the Church of England. Wesley was sorry. He had wanted to revive the Church of England, not to divide it.

He did revive it in a way which he did not live to see. About a hundred years after Wesley and Whitefield had been students at Oxford, another group of students met in their rooms at the same university to see how what Wesley had done for the English poor could be done for the bulk of those in the English Church. They felt, as Wesley had done, that the Enlightenment had lost some of the great parts of Christianity. Wesley had recovered the warmth and purity. They wanted to recover also the faith and beauty. The Enlightenment, they said, had pruned the Christian faith altogether too much and had forgotten that God is not so simple. He is great, holy and tremendous. The old creeds of the Church alone set forth the richness of God. And Puritanism, they thought, had destroyed the beauty of religion by removing everything from the services practised by the Church of Rome. The

Oxford students loved to imagine the Church in England as it had been in the Middle Ages, when, as the poet Sir Walter Scott wrote:

> And slow up the dim aisle afar,
> With sable cowl and scapular,
> And snow-white stoles, in order due,
> The holy fathers, two and two,
> In long procession came;
> Taper, and Host, and book they bare,
> And holy banner, flourished fair
> With the Redeemer's name.
> Then mass was sung, and prayers were said,
> And solemn requiem for the dead;
> And bells tolled out their mighty peal
> For the departed spirit's weal;
> And ever in the office close
> The hymn of intercession rose;
> And far the echoing aisles prolong
> The awful burthen of the song,—
> > Dies irae, dies illa,
> > Solvet sæclum in favilla.
> > [*Day of judgment, day of ire,*
> > *When the world dissolves in fire.*]

But if the Church of England should go back to so many of the beliefs and practices of the Church of Rome why not go back to the Church of Rome itself and not have any Church of England any more? This was what John Henry Newman came to think. He joined the Roman Catholic Church. Most of the Oxford Group, however, did not agree with him. To be a Catholic, said they, and

to recover the faith and beauty of the Catholic Church, one does not need to be a Roman Catholic. One can be an English Catholic. They call themselves Anglo-Catholics, which means English Catholics.

As the English Church had been in need of revival in Wesley's day so a century later Methodism itself was in need of revival. The great-grandchildren of the first poor Methodists had grown too prosperous to care greatly for the poor of their own day. Yet the Methodist Church still had enough of the spirit of Wesley to make more men who were like him. One was William Booth, the founder of the Salvation Army. He is supposed to have said, "There is one God and John Wesley is His prophet." As Wesley went to England's poor at the mouths of the coal pits Booth found them in London's slums. As Wesley used boulders for pulpits Booth used curbstones. The Methodist leaders called Booth to a conference and told him that he must settle in a church and give only half his time to the poor. His wife Catherine, who was there, called to him, "Never, William! Never!"

Together they started a movement after Wesley's own heart. And they did more than preach to the poor. They started soup kitchens, shelters for the men sleeping on the bridges, homes for girls in trouble. And Booth woke up all England by a book called *In Darkest England*. A book had just come out with the title, *In Darkest Africa*. Booth showed that England was darker still.

As Wesley had taken lay preachers so Booth took those who were won and put them right to work winning others. Zeal mattered more than book learning. Once a fisherman was preaching on the story of Jesus in which the servant said to his master, "Lord, I feared thee because thou art an austere man." The fisherman thought it was "oyster man," and told how the oyster fishermen had to get wet and dirty and cut their hands on the shells to win the oysters. So Jesus suffered to win men. Twelve men were won that night and when the mistake was pointed out to the fisherman he said, "Never mind! We got twelve oysters."

The name for the new movement was chosen by one of the members. He suggested the Salvation Army. The name took and then the workers were called sergeants, corporals, captains and majors. William Booth did not quite like being "General," but he had to accept the title given him. He made the flag, a base of red for the blood of Christ, a border of blue for holiness, a center of yellow for the fire of the Spirit. The motto was Blood and Fire. The Salvation Army had a band or at least cornet, drum and cymbals. They marched and played and sang and shouted "Hallelujah." When Booth died the poet Vachel Lindsay wrote these verses to be sung to the ever softer and slower beating of the drum—

Booth died blind and still by Faith he trod,
Eyes still dazzled by the ways of God.
Booth led boldly, and he looked the chief
Eagle countenance in sharp relief,
Beard a-flying, air of high command
Unabated in that holy land.

CHAPTER TWENTY-TWO

A NEW WORLD

MERICA, when discovered, opened up a new field for the Church. Here was a *Terra Nova*, which means a new earth. Full of terrors the map maker of the Old World imagined it and put all the cannibals and monsters which you see above in the center of his map. Yet for all the terrors here was a world with new men to be won for Christ and new lands where the persecuted could find freedom.

First came the explorers, later the colonists. For the first hundred years after the discovery of America the efforts of the Church were bent on converting the Indians. After 1600, white settlers began to fill up the land and brought with them different forms of religion from the Old World. We shall look first at the missionaries to the Indians and then at the colonists and their churches.

Christopher Columbus on reaching the shores of the New World raised the cross of Christ and the flag of Spain and wrote to the King that the natives "have a knowledge that there is a

God above and are firmly persuaded that we come from heaven."
They should be Christianized, he added, and the King would
receive much gold from the country. Unfortunately the conquerors cared most for the gold. They would baptize the Indians
to save their souls and then rob and enslave their bodies. Here is

Cortez the bloody conqueror of Mexico holding up the crucifix
while Indian chiefs are being baptized. The circle in the priest's
hand is the bowl from which he is pouring water. The belief of
the natives that the newcomers came from heaven was used to
trick them. The white men offered the simple folk a voyage
to paradise to see their dead forefathers, but once on board the
Indians were carried into slavery.

Real Christians were shocked by such cruelty. A Dominican
friar named Las Casas wrote an account of the barbarities and
went home to Spain to put the case before the King. The Spaniards asked Las Casas how much he thought could be done with
the Indians without swords and only with words. He replied that
he would go into a fierce region called the Land of War and

would win it to Christ by words alone provided the King would keep all other Spaniards away for five years. Las Casas did it and changed the name of that land to Vera Paz, the Land of True Peace. It is today a part of Guatemala.

In Mexico and Southern California, the Franciscans were active. Here is a picture of two of their missionaries meeting an Indian chief and his three squaws. San Francisco is named for Saint Francis. Los Angeles means The Angels. Sacramento means The Sacrament.

In the North, along the St. Lawrence and the Great Lakes, the

Jesuits were the most outstanding missionaries. Among their number none was more brave and good than Isaac Jogues. He was a French lad. His mother, at Orleans in France, heard him say his first Mass and bade him good-bye as he sailed for the New World. "I do not know what it is to enter paradise," he wrote his mother, "but I cannot imagine a greater joy than was mine when I said Mass at Quebec." Then he set out to work among the Hurons. A father who had been with them before gave him this advice, "You must have real love for the savages. Do not keep them waiting when they get in their boats. Light their pipes for them and their fires. Eat their food, even if you don't like it, and take it at the time when it is served. Do not carry sand or water into their canoes. Make no trouble and don't ask too many questions. Do not criticize. Always be cheerful. Give them pocket knives, fish-hooks, and glass beads. Carry their baggage, if it be only a kettle. They care nothing for the qualities which made you loved in France. If you could go naked and carry as much as a horse, they would think you a great man. Think only on the cross of Christ and you shall find roses in thorns and sweetness in bitterness."

Among the Hurons, Father Jogues and his fellow "Black Robes" as the Indians called them, were in danger because they got well after an attack of influenza, whereas many Indians died. The Hurons thought the whites must have some magic which they used only for themselves. When at last the trust of the Hurons was won, another trouble came. The Mohawks were at war with the Hurons and the French. Some one was needed to go back from the mission to Quebec for supplies. Jogues was asked, though not ordered, to go. He went with some companions, both French and Indian, but the party was ambushed. The soldiers fought manfully. Jogues, as a priest, was not allowed to fight and lay hidden in the grass. He might have run away, but he said, "Could I leave our French and the Christian Indians when they needed me to give them the help of the Church in their tortures?" He gave himself up.

Some of his companions were frightfully tortured and killed. His life was spared because the Mohawks wanted him in bargaining with the French, but, while sparing his life, the Indians tore out his fingernails, cut off his left thumb, and reduced some of his fingers to stumps. At night he was chained on the ground while Indian children put hot coals upon his body.

At last he was rescued by the Dutch and was given the kindest care by a Presbyterian minister. Father Jogues then went home to France and on Christmas Day saw his mother again. But he longed to return to the Mohawks who had treated him so ill. "If I am employed in this mission," he wrote, "my heart tells me I shall not return. It will be well for me if God will be pleased to complete the sacrifice there where He began it, if the little blood which I shed there in that land will be accepted by Him as a pledge that I would willingly shed all. Our good Master who gained this people for Himself, by His own blood, may open to it the door of the Gospel." Father Jogues returned to fall under a tomahawk.

The Dutch who saved him on an earlier occasion were colonists, one group among the many which filled up the Atlantic seaboard during the seventeenth century. The colonists came to the New World only in part for reasons of religion. Some wished a place where they might worship God as they thought right. Others were looking for a chance to make an easier living. But whatever the reason, most of them carried over the idea that only one religion could be allowed in one place. In most of the colonies Church and State were united and only that form of Christianity which was united with the State was permitted. In Pennsylvania and Maryland, though Church and State were not united, yet not every form of religion was allowed. Rhode Island was the first to have a complete separation of Church and State.

If we go up the Atlantic coast from the south we find that the southern colonies, particularly Virginia, were Episcopalian. The Catholics founded Maryland, the Quakers Pennsylvania, the Presbyterians New Jersey and New York, the Congregationalists Connecticut and Massachusetts, and the Baptists Rhode Island. We shall look at these in turn.

In Virginia the Episcopalians settled. Captain John Smith, their leader, thus describes the first church:

"When first we went to Virginia I well remember we did hang an awning (which is an old sail) to three or four trees, to shadow us from the sun; our walls were rails of wood; our seats unhewed trees till we cut planks; our pulpit a bar of wood nailed to two neighboring trees. In foul weather we shifted into an old rotten tent.

"This was our church till we built a homely thing like a barn, set upon cratchets, covered with rafts sedge and earth; so was the walls. The best of our houses of like curiosity, but the most part far much worse workmanship, that neither could well defend wind nor rain. Yet we had daily Common Prayer, morning and evening; every Sunday two sermons; and every three months the holy Communion."

When Lord Delaware came in 1610, a better church was built, of which we have this account:

"The Captain General hath given order for the repairing of the church and at this instant many hands are about it. It is in length three-score foot, in breadth twenty-four, and shall have a Chancel in it of cedar, and a Communion table of the black walnut, and all the pews of cedar, with fair broad windows, to shut and open, as the weather shall occasion, of the same wood, a pulpit of the same, with a font hewn hollow, like a canoe, with two bells at the west end. It is so cast, as to be very light within, and the Lord Governor and Captain General doth cause it to be kept passing sweet, and trimmed up with divers flowers, with a

Sexton belonging to it; and in it every Sunday we have sermons twice a day, and every Thursday a sermon, having two preachers, which take their weekly turns; and every morning at the ringing of a bell, about ten of the clock, each man addresseth himself to prayers, and so at four of the clock before supper. Every Sunday, when the Lord Governor and Captain General goeth to Church, he is accompanied with all the Counselors, Captains, other officers and all the gentlemen, with a guard of Halberdiers, in his Lordship's livery, fair red cloaks, to the number of fifty both on each side, and behind him; and being in the Church his Lordship hath his seat in the choir, in a green velvet chair, with a cloth, with a velvet cushion spread on a table before him, on which he kneeleth, and on each side sit the Council, Captains, and officers each in their place, and when he returneth home again, he is waited on to his house in the same manner."

The Episcopal Church was for long the only Church in Virginia. George Washington belonged to this Church.

Delaware was settled by Swedish Lutherans. They had great difficulty in getting ministers from the old country and even to get word home, but at length they were able to reach an officer of the King with a letter saying: "We do heartily desire that there may be sent unto us two Swedish ministers, who are well learned in the Holy Scriptures so that we may preserve our true Lutheran faith. Further, it is our humble desire that you would be pleased to send us three books of sermons, twelve Bibles, forty-two psalm books, one hundred tracts, with two hundred catechisms, and as many primers; for which, when received, we promise punctual payment at such place as you may think fit to order.

"As to what concerns our situation in this country, we are for the most part husbandmen. We plough and sow, and till the

ground; and as to our meat and drink, we live according to the
old Swedish custom. We live also in peace and friendship with
one another; and the Indians have not molested us for many years.
We have always had over us good and gracious magistrates; and
we live with one another in peace and quietness. So that we desire,
as soon as this our letter comes to hand, that a speedy attention
may be paid to our request; for we believe that God has certainly
his hand in this Christian work, and pray that he may bring it
to a happy termination."

In response to this letter the King of Sweden and his Archbishop sent three Swedish Lutheran ministers to Delaware. This
was in the year 1696.

Maryland was founded by a Catholic, Lord Baltimore, who
wished a place of refuge for those of his religion who were persecuted in some countries of Europe. The Catholic Church, however, was not united with the State in Maryland, and was not the
only Church allowed. The Catholics were not even a majority in
the colony. In other colonies there were scarcely any Catholics.
The great strength of the Catholic Church in this country did
not come until later, as we shall see.

In Pennsylvania the Quakers found a home. The state was
named for William Penn. He was the son of the Admiral of
the Fleet in England, who was very vexed when his son took off
his sword, kept on his hat and dressed in the plain fashion of the
Friends. On the following page are some pictures of American
Friends showing their costume. The old Admiral disowned his son
at first, but could not help admiring him for giving up the ease of
the King's court to lie in a vile prison. The father had still more
reason to be proud when the son so stirred an English jury that,
after being kept without food, warmth or any comfort for two

days and nights by the judge to make them find Penn guilty, yet on the second morning, tired and dirty, they still came back with the answer "Not guilty." Admiral Penn put William back in his will and that was how he came to have the wealth and standing to start

a colony in the New World for the Quakers. In all his dealings with the Indians he was just. He made a treaty with them which was never sworn to by an oath and never broken. Many other persecuted groups in Holland and Germany found a home with the Quakers, such as the Mennonites, Schwenckfelders, and Dunkards.

A letter from a Quaker girl in Pennsylvania to her grandmother in England has been saved. Here is a part of it:

The Manor, Bucks County, Pa.
The 28th of 11th Mo., 1685

Dear Grandmother:

Mamma has been writing to thee since last Fifth-day, and she told me I could put a sheet into thy letter. We want to get it off on the packet which sails from Philadelphia about the 10th of the Twelfth month.

Our new house is all done. I wish thee could see our big kitchen. It has a fireplace entirely across one end of the room. Papa brings the back log in with the horse, and when the boys pile wood up against it, such a fire as it does make. We have so much wood. Papa says we would be rich if we had this timber in England. I gather chips. We had a nice time roasting chestnuts this fall in the ashes. I have four quarts dried.

The new house is built of logs and all nicely plastered inside. We'll be good and warm this winter. We have a Dutch oven now.

I wish thee could have seen our garden this summer. Besides the rows of sage, camomile, thyme, comfrey and rue, with yarrow and some onions, we have great big love apples [tomatoes]. They are almost as large as an apple. They grow on a bushy plant which starts from a seed in the spring. Uncle Henry found them last summer among the Indians, and brought some of the seeds home. Mamma says they are poison if we eat them. They are just pretty to look at.

We have so many horses and cows that are not ours. Papa is Ranger now, and takes up all strays. Thee don't know about this, does thee? Well, everybody here lets their cows and horses run loose in the woods. Sometimes they don't come back, and it takes a long time to find them. We heard of a little girl this fall who got lost while hunting for the cows. Dark came on and she heard the wolves howling. It was very late when she found the cows all huddled together. Her father found her next morning fast asleep alongside of the bell cow. She was safe and sound. I'm glad I wasn't that little girl.

Mamma has school for me every day. She is the teacher and I am the scholars. I am head of my class. Papa says that if I keep on doing that well he will send me to England to school when I get big. Then I'll see thee, grandma, and the dear old place I love so well. There is no more room on the paper, so I must stop.

With lots of kisses and two pats for dear old Rover, I remain thy affectionate granddaughter,

Sally Brindley.

In New Jersey and New York the Presbyterian Church took the lead. The first settlers were the Dutch, whose Church, called the Dutch Reformed, is a branch of the Presbyterian system. When the English took the colony over, Lord Cornbury tried to force the people to go to the Episcopal Church. Francis Makemie, the Presbyterian minister, refused, and held the service in a house. He was brought up for trial and was asked:

"Do you own you preached and baptized a child at the home of so-and-so?"

"Yes."

"How many hearers did you have?"

"I have got more to do than to count them."

"More than five?"

"Yes, and five more."

"Did you have leave from Lord Cornbury?"

"Leave was asked for me."

Makemie pointed out that the Apostles, Peter and Paul, did not ask leave of any one to preach. Makemie won because by this time the laws of England allowed more than one religion in the old country and the colony of New York could not be stricter than the mother land.

In Connecticut and Massachusetts the Congregationalists settled. Some of them had gone from England to Holland. Their children were growing up Dutch and the parents wanted to go to a place where they would be free to worship God in their own way and rear their children as Englishmen. They sailed on the *Mayflower* and landed at Plymouth Rock near Boston. Forty-eight men came; during the first winter, twenty-eight died. Yet when the ship sailed back to England in the spring, none of the settlers went with her. This was in 1621. Soon more colonists came and settled Boston, and, by and by, New Haven and Hartford in Connecticut. Only Congregational churches were allowed for a long time in Massachusetts and Connecticut.

The Baptists were not permitted to settle in Massachusetts, and Roger Williams, their leader, was put out partly because he was a Baptist, and partly because he said that the government should not control religion. Governor Winslow of Plymouth told Williams to go into the open country and be as free as the Congregationalists and a good neighbor. A better time of the year might have been chosen for such advice, for he was sent away in the midst of a New England winter. He called the town which he founded Providence. Others of like mind founded other towns in the neighborhood. These united to form the State of Rhode Island. It was the first colony to separate completely Church and State. Roger Williams secured from King Charles II in England this agreement:

"Our royal will and pleasure is that no person within the said colony, at any time hereafter, shall be any wise molested, punished, disquieted, or called in question, for any differences in opinion in matters of religion, who do not actually disturb the civil peace of our said colony; but that all and every person and persons may, from time to time, and at all times hereafter, freely and fully have and enjoy his and their own judgments and consciences in matters of religious concernments, throughout the tract of land hereafter mentioned; they behaving themselves peaceably and quietly."

New Haven, Connecticut, 1786

CHAPTER
TWENTY–THREE

FREEDOM'S HOLY LIGHT

HE example of Rhode Island in the separation of Church and State began to be followed by other colonies and in the year of the Revolutionary War the Virginia Bill of Rights said, "That religion, or the duty which we owe to our Creator, and the manner of discharging it, can be directed only by reason and conviction, not by force or violence; and therefore all men are equally entitled to the free exercise of religion, according to the dictates of conscience; and that it is the mutual duty of all to practise Christian forbearance, love, and charity towards each other." When the colonies formed the United States of America the Constitution in 1787 declared that "Congress shall make no law respecting an establishment of religion, or prohibiting the free exercise thereof." The Constitution, however, did not say that the individual states must do the same and some of them continued for a time in the old ways. In the early years of the nineteenth century, however, Church and State came to be separated everywhere in America. No one Church is anywhere favored more than another. Every Church and every man and woman is free to worship God in the way which seems right.

The separation of Church and State does not mean, however, that the United States is not interested in religion. There are chaplains in the national Congress and in the state legislatures. Sunday, Thanksgiving and Christmas are legal holidays. Lands and buildings used for Church purposes pay no taxes. The American dollar, quarter and dime bear the words "In God We Trust." When Theodore Roosevelt was President he thought that coins were not the best places for religious mottoes and tried to have them taken off, but Congress refused.

The United States has welcomed to its shores those of all faiths and because of the separation of Church and State they have been able to settle freely in any part of the country. We shall glance first at some of the groups which have become strong because of the numbers which have come from abroad, and next at the churches which have sprung up on this side of the water. Then we shall notice what the churches have meant to American life.

The Lutherans in the early period did not come in large numbers. The Swedes on the Delaware were but a small group and the colony soon passed to the English. In later years the German Lutherans came in larger groups and formed strong settlements especially in Pennsylvania and still later in Missouri. The Scandinavian Lutherans formed the backbone of Minnesota.

The Catholics increased at first mainly because of the misfortunes of Ireland which had grown more and more attached to the Roman Catholic Church out of hatred for the misrule of Protestant England. Other disasters such as war and famine drove the Irish to seek a home abroad. During the nineteenth century waves of Italians and Poles came to this country and they, too, were for the most part Catholic.

The Methodists were here before the Revolution. This ship

sailed with some of them in 1760. Philip Embury, founder of the first Methodist church in the States, is shown preaching from the deck. The Methodists were not in time to found a colony and that was probably an advantage, because arriving late they went everywhere. While Congregational, Presbyterian and Baptist ministers lived in parsonages, Methodists lived in saddlebags. On horseback, like John Wesley, they covered the coast from Georgia to Maine and when the West opened went far across the plains. A glimpse of the travels and preaching of George Whitefield in this country is given by a farmer of Middletown, Connecticut. He writes:

"Now it pleased God to send Mr. Whitefield into this land and my hearing of his preaching at Philadelphia like one of the old apostles and many thousands flocking after him to hear the Gospel and great numbers were converted to Christ, I felt the spirit of God drawing me by conviction. I longed to see and hear him and wished he would come this way and I soon heard he was come to New York and the Jersies and great multitudes flocking after him under great concern for their souls and many converted which brought on my concern more and more, hoping soon to see him but next I heard he was on Long Island and next at Boston and next at Northampton, and then one morning all on a sudden about 8 or 9 o'clock, there came a messenger and said Mr. Whitefield preached at Hartford and Wethersfield yesterday and is to preach at Middletown this morning at 10 o'clock. I was in my field at work. I dropt my tool that I had in my hand and ran home and ran through my house and had my wife get ready quick to go and hear Mr. Whitefield preach at Middletown and ran to my pasture for my horse with all my might fearing I should be too late to hear him. I brought my horse home and soon mounted and took my wife up and went forward as fast as I thought the horse could bear and when my horse began to be out of breath I would get down and put my wife on the saddle and bid her ride as fast as she could and not stop or slack for me except I bade her and so I would run until I was almost out of breath and then mount my horse again and so I did several times to favor my horse. We improved every moment to get along as if we were fleeing for our lives, all this while fearing we should be too late to hear the sermon for we had twelve miles to ride double in little more than an hour and we went round by the upper parish and when we came within half a mile of the road that comes down from Hartford, Wethersfield, and Stepney to Middletown on

high land I saw before me a cloud or fog rising, I first thought
off from the Great River but as I came nearer the road I heard
a noise something like a low rumbling thunder and I presently
found it was the rumbling of horses feet coming down the road,
and this cloud was a cloud of dust made by the running of horses
feet, it arose some rods into the air over the tops of the hills and
trees and when I came within about twenty rods of the road I
could see men and horses slipping along in the cloud like shadows
and when I came nearer it was like a steady stream of horses, and
their riders, scarcely a horse more than his length behind another,
all of a lather and foam with sweat, their breath rolling out of
their nostrils, in a cloud of dust every jump, every horse seemed
to go with all his might to carry his ri'er to hear the news from
Heaven to the saving of their souls. It made me tremble to see
the sight how the world was in a struggle. I found a vacance
between two horses to slip in my horse and my wife said, 'Law,
our clothes will be all spoiled, see how they look'—for they was

so covered with dust they looked almost all of a color, coats and hats and shirts and horses. We went down in the stream. I heard no man speak a word all the way, three miles, but every one pressing forward in great haste and when we got down to the old meeting-house there was a great multitude, it was said to be 3 or 4000 of people assembled together. We got off from our horses and shook off the dust and the ministers was then coming to the meeting-house. I turned and looked toward the Great River and saw the ferry boats running swift forward and backward bringing over loads of people, the oars rowed nimble and quick; everything, men, horses and boats seemed to be struggling for life; the land and the banks over the river looked black with people and horses. All along the twelve miles I see no man at work in his field but all seemed to be gone. When I see Mr. Whitefield come up upon the scaffold he looked almost angelical, a young slim slender youth before some thousands of people and with a bold undaunted countenance. And my hearing how God was with him everywhere as he came along it solemnized my mind and put me in a trembling fear before he began to preach for he looked as if he was clothed with authority from the great God and a sweet solemn Solemnity sat upon his brow, and my hearing him preach gave me a heart wound by God's blessing."

The Lutherans, Catholics and Methodists thus spread partly because of those who came from abroad, partly by those who were won over here.

New religious groups sprang up in this country. The Disciples of Christ separated from the Presbyterians because of the belief that if only all the Churches would go back to the exact pattern of the New Testament all the Churches would be one. The Disciples tried to show the way.

The Unitarians broke off from the Congregationalists. There were to be sure Unitarians already in England, but in this country the members of the Unitarian Churches came out of the Congregational. As the name suggests the Unitarians believe that God is a Unity and not a Trinity. They are not willing to call Jesus actually God. They say that he is like God and we should try to be like him, having his spirit of love, service and peace. The Unitarians have taken the lead in working for the peace of the world.

The Mormons sprang up entirely in this country. They believe that ten of the twelve tribes of Israel carried away into captivity came over to South America and there had a history much like that of the two tribes in Palestine. The story is told in *The Book of Mormon*. This Church is also called The Church of the Latter Day Saints. Some settled in Missouri and some in Utah.

Christian Science also began in America. It teaches that evil and sickness are not real and if people believe strongly enough in goodness and health they will not be sick. The Christian Scientists carry on one of our best newspapers—*The Christian Science Monitor*.

In the early days in America the Church was the center of the community. In the heart of the village was the green and in the middle of the green was the church. The church, apart from the town meeting, was all that brought the entire community

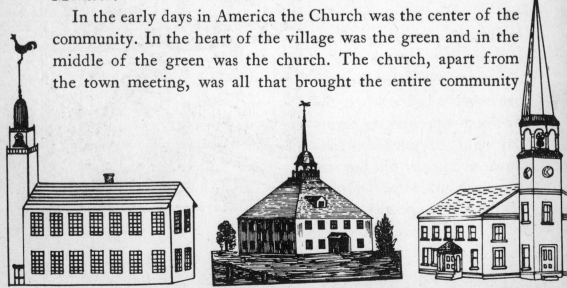

together. We shall notice how the churches were built and how the Sabbath was kept.

The church buildings in the colonies were very plain meeting-houses, square in shape with a pyramid roof, topped by a belfry. The oldest building of this type still standing in the same place and still used for worship is the one at Hingham, Massachusetts, built in 1681. Later churches of the Christopher Wren type were built on this side of the water but with changes to make them fit Puritan ideas. No cross, only a weathercock, was allowed on the spire. The pulpit, not the altar, was the center of interest, and sometimes in order to be as different as possible from Catholic and Episcopal churches the pulpit was placed in the middle of the long wall with the main door opposite as in the church at North ampton, Massachusetts. In the course of time narrow Puritan views passed away and the pulpit was put back at the end of the long way of the building.

On the inside of the churches the seats were sometimes pews in rows and sometimes square boxes without a lid, in which children could be heard but not seen. This picture shows a boy and his sister left by themselves in one of these box pews. He has been misbehaving and she is giving him a lecture.

Sunday was called the Sabbath and began when the first star appeared on Saturday night and ended with sundown on Sunday. The day was strictly kept. Some children found it tiresome and had to be scolded by the Justice of the Peace for "rude and idle behavior in the meeting house such as smiling and laughing and enticing others to the evil." One lad was reproved for "throwing Sister Pentecost Perkins on the ice it being Sabbath day between the meeting house and his place of abode."

But Sunday, all in all, was not such a terrible day and those who grew up taking it for granted loved the day for its grave and simple charm. Henry Ward Beecher, a Congregational minister and the son of one, tells how the day was kept when he was a boy. Everything needful was made ready the day before. When Sunday came every one walked softly, spoke in a low tone. "Yet all were cheerful. The cook was blacker than ever. The coffee better, the cream richer, and the broiled chickens juicier and more tender; and the biscuit whiter and the corn bread more brittle and sweet."

When the day dawned all was quiet in the town. "The saw was ripping away yesterday in the carpenter's shop and the hammer was noisy enough. Today there is not a sign of life there. The anvil makes no music today. The mill is silent. Only the brook continues noisy. And the birds are all singing—larks, robins, blackbirds, orioles, sparrows, and bluebirds; mocking catbirds and wrens, singing as on no other day but Sunday when other sounds are still.

"There was no sound in the village store. Look either way—not a wagon; not a human being. The smoke rose up soberly and quietly as if it said, 'It's Sunday.' The leaves on the great elms, hung motionless, glittering in the dew, as if they too were waiting for the bell to ring for meeting, and when the first bell rang, the sound rolled over and over through the air, twice as far as on week days. There were no less than seven steeples in sight from the belfry, and the sexton said when the wind was right he had heard all seven.

"At meeting time the empty streets suddenly were filled but there was no fevered hurry. All blossomed in their best like a rosebud in June. Do you know that man in the silk hat and new

black coat? Probably it is some stranger. No, it is the carpenter who was racing about yesterday with his sleeves rolled up and a dust and business look in his face. And there's the blacksmith— does he not look every inch a judge now that he is clean washed, shaved and dressed? His eyes are as bright as the sparks that fly from his anvil."

In the church all forgot the labors and the cares of the week as they sang the psalms and took comfort in the promises of the God who guarded Israel through the wilderness and had led their exiled fathers to the "stern and rock bound coast" where in freedom they might worship Him.

The Churches have done much for the United States. Without them for many a long year there would have been no education at all. Public education in the beginning was entirely given by the Churches. And religion was taught in the schools. *The New England Primer* had this verse:

> The Praises of my tongue
> I offer to the Lord
> That I was taught and learned so young
> To read his Holy Word.

The separation of Church and State meant that the State raised the money for the schools, but did not mean that religion was to be taken out of the teaching. The Churches founded most of the colleges before the state universities began. The Congregationalists founded Harvard, Yale, Williams, Dartmouth, Bowdoin, Amherst, Middlebury, Mount Holyoke, Smith, Wheaton, and Wellesley—all these in the East, and in the Middle and Far West Oberlin and Whitman; the Methodists have founded Duke, Emory, Vanderbilt, DePauw, Randolph-Macon, Goucher, Wesleyan in Connecticut and Wesleyan in Ohio; the Lutherans have to their credit Gettysburg in Pennsylvania, Concordia, St. Olaf and Augsburg in Minnesota, Augustana in Illinois and Northwestern College in Wisconsin; the Presbyterian and Reformed started Princeton, Washington and Lee, and Rutgers; the Episcopalians William and Mary, and Columbia; the Baptists Vassar and Brown; the Quakers Bryn Mawr, Swarthmore and Haverford; the Disciples Bethany, Hiram and Drake; the Catholics Fordham, Notre Dame and the Catholic University at Washington. And this is by no means all. Most of these colleges are no longer managed by the churches, but the teaching is still touched by religion.

The churches have striven manfully against the evils of our land. One evil was duelling. Men used to think it right to settle their quarrels by fighting with swords or pistols. The killing of Alexander Hamilton by Aaron Burr in this way was a great shock and stirred the ministers to speak out roundly in favor of settling quarrels by law in the courts instead of by swords or pistols in the fields.

Another great evil was slavery. Cheap labor was desired for the cotton plantations in the South. The Indians had been largely killed off. Slave traders, many of them from New England, stirred up wars between the tribes of Negroes in Africa and made slaves of the prisoners, packing them like sardines in the ships to be brought over and sold in America. The Quakers first came to the view that slave-holding is wrong. John Wesley spoke most sharply against the slave trade. The Churches stirred up the conscience of the country against the inhumanity of slavery. When the

slaves ran away the newspapers in the slave-holding states carried these pictures urging that the slaves be caught and returned. Some church people instead helped them to make good their escape through what was called the "underground railway," really a string of houses where slaves could lodge and be hidden on their way to the free states. The Civil War was fought largely over slavery. Some of the Churches were unhappily divided by the war such as the Baptists, Methodists and Presbyterians into a southern and a northern branch. The Methodists have since come together again.

Still another evil was drunkenness, which wasted the money, destroyed the health, and wrecked the family of many a good man. Church people did not at first object to drinking and even church gatherings were often disorderly through taking too much. A Quaker doctor, during the Revolutionary War, saw so much of

the dreaded effects of liquor that he came out with a tract called *Inquiry Into the Effects of Ardent Spirits upon the Human Mind and Body*. He showed that alcohol is not necessary to heat the body in cold nor to strengthen it in hot weather. In a little over half a century 200,000 copies of his tract were sold and temperance societies were formed to teach people to be temperate in the use of liquor. Tracts were printed with woodcuts like the above, showing the model farm where the bottle is not welcome.

One of the noblest works of the Church has been the carrying the news of Jesus and his love to lands which have never heard of him. Just as in the Middle Ages men like Boniface and Ansgar carried the news to England and Germany, so in our days great hosts of missionaries have gone out to the ends of the earth. Another book larger than this one would be needed even to begin to tell the stories of such men as Livingstone in Africa, Carey in India, Judson in Burma and Schweitzer in Africa in the nineteenth and twentieth centuries. Already Christian Churches are firmly grounded in India, Africa, Japan and China. They have reached the point where their members are able to stand upon their own feet and need the missionary now more as a teacher and friend than as a founder and controller of their Churches. Christianity is taking on new forms in the minds of the brown and yellow and black men and Christ in their pictures is shown as one of themselves and not always as a white man. The Light of the World is burning on a Chinese candlestick.

The end of this book is not the end of this story.

The Church we hope will carry on her work of healing for mankind throughout the long, long years to come. Often in the past she has been sorely tried. Often she has sadly failed. But the voice of Jesus has always called her again to serve him. The words which little Sarah Bancroft stitched into her sampler when our land was new carry us back through the years to the prophet of Israel who spoke them centuries before Christ and these same words carry us forward as far as the mind can reach. They can never fail because they are the Word of God.

PICTURES, BOOKS AND HELPERS

The pictures in this book were taken from originals often quite faint or too large and complicated to be used as they were. For that reason most of them had to be redrawn. The task was simplified and lightened through a process worked out by Paul Graybill, formerly director of the Visual Education Department of the Works Progress Administration in New Haven, Conn. The process consists in making from a Leica snapshot an enlargement on which the main lines are traced over with waterproof ink. The photograph is then faded out entirely and details are put in free hand from the original.

In many instances only a portion of the picture has been used. The tug of war on p. 109 for example is a detail from an elaborate drawing of the Judgment Day by Alart du Hameel (in Elfred Bock, *Geschichte der graphischen Kunst,* 1930). Sometimes a hand or a foot or even a face if indistinct or missing has been drawn in. The sketch of Geneva on p. 161, which was redrawn by Herbert Woodruff Bainton from a sixteenth-century woodcut, was retouched by the omission of a hill and river in the background, which obscured the skyline of the city, and also by making the walls white and the roofs black for contrast. The only serious liberty was taken in the case of the singers on p. 149. In the original no one was pumping the organ.

Only some of the more important books from which pictures were taken can be noted. Most of the Goliath pictures on p. 3 are from Theodor Ehrenstein, *Das Alte Testament im Bilde* (1923). Most of the initial letters are from Oscar Jennings, *Woodcut Initials* (1908). Several cuts came from A. M. Hind, *History of Woodcut* (1935). A brief list of other books is given on the next page.

In the modern period for England and America the pictures are not infrequently taken directly from the tracts of the time. The drawing of Charles I, for example, on p. 189 is from John Taylor's *England's Comfort (Spenser Society,* 1867). Several of the American cuts are from the publications of the American Tract Society.

I am indebted to Frederick Norwood for help in collecting pictures and to Harlan Lewis for redrawing several. My wife is a never-failing source of counsel. The staff of the Yale Library is indefatigable in assistance. Members of the staff of Charles Scribner's Sons, Miss Dalgliesh, Mr.

Dymock, and Mr. Savage, have given me no end of help. Joyce Bainton assisted in making the index and Cedric and Ruth Bainton (aged nine and seven) in arranging the index entries in alphabetical order.

Quotations in the text with free modification of spelling and sometimes language are taken as follows from: p. 103, E. P. Cubberley, *Readings in the History of Education* (1920); p. 116, *The Chester Miracle Plays* (ed. I. and O. Bolton King, 1930); p. 104, *The Nun's Rule* (ed. James Morton, 1905); p. 188, *The King's Maiesties Declaration . . . concerning Lawful Sports* (1618); pp. 146–47, Arthur C. McGiffert, *Martin Luther* (1911); pp. 172–73, *Ballads from Manuscripts* (ed. F. J. Furnivall, 1868–76); pp. 221–22, Edward L. Goodwin, *The Colonial Church in Virginia* (1927); p. 224, Isaac Sharpless, *A Quaker Experiment in Government* (1898); pp. 231–33, Ellen D. Larned, *Historic Gleanings in Windham County, Conn.* (1899), also in George Leon Walker, *Some Aspects of the Religious Life of New England* (1897).

Among the more important works used for the pictures are the following: E. S. Bolton, *American Samplers* (1921); G. G. Coulton, *Five Centuries of Religion* (1923–36), and *Art and the Reformation* (1928); *Dictionnaire d'archéologie Chrétienne* (1907–   ); A. N. Didron, *Christian Iconography* (1886); J. Dominguez Bordona, *Spanish Illumination* (1930); E. Doumergue, *Iconographie Calvinienne* (1909); P. Drews, *Der Evangelische Geistliche* (1905); E. Droz, *Livres à Gravures Imprimés à Lyon* (1926); H. Fehr, *Massenkunst im 16. Jahrhundert* (1924); J. B. G. Galiffe, *Genève Historique* (1869); H. Gardner, *Art Through the Ages* (1926); Max Geisberg, *Die Reformation* (1929), and *Die Deutsche Buchillustration* (1930–   ); *The Guthlac Roll* (ed. G. Warner, 1928); *Graphic Arts* (1936); D. Hartley, *Life and Work of the People of England*, III (1926); P. Heitz, *Genfer Buchdrucker* (1908); A. D. Innes, *History of the British Nation* (1912); Mrs. Jameson, *Sacred and Legendary Art* (1905); C. M. Kaufmann, *Handbuch der Christlichen Archäologie* (1913); H. Kehrer, *Die Heiligen Drei Könige* (1909); N. P. Kondakov, *The Russian Icon* (1927); A. G. Little, *Franciscan History* (1937); W. Lowrie, *Monuments* (1901); *Luttrell Psalter* (ed. G. Millar, 1932); F. W. Madden, *Coins of the Jews* (1881); H. Martin, *La Miniature Française* (1923); O. Marucchi, *Manual of Christian Archeology* (1935); G. Millet, *Monuments de l'Athos* (1927); S. Morison, *Modern Fine Printing* (1925); *National Geographic* LXXVIII (1940); *Old-Time New England* (1922–23 and 1930); C. Oursel, *La Miniature du XIIIe Siècle* (1926); A. Parmentier, *Album Historique* (1909); J. R. Allen, *Early Christian Symbolism* (1887); A. Saba, *Storia dei Papi* (1936); Luigi Salvatorelli, *L'Italia Medioevale* (1938); *Schools of Illumination* (1926); A. Schramm, *Bilderschmuck der Frühdrucke* (1920–   ); Paul Schreckenbach, *Martin Luther* (1916); H. Y. Thompson, *Illustrations from 100 Manuscripts* (1916); H. D. Traill and J. S. Mann, *The Building of Britain* V (1909); A. S. Turberville, *English Men and Manners* (1932); F. R. Webber, *Church Symbolism* (1927); Thomas Wright, *History of Caricature* (1865); Oskar Wulff, *Altchristliche und Byzantinische Kunst* (1914).

INDEX

(Figures in parenthesis indicate dates)